HANGING ON BY
MY FINGERNAILS

Praise for Janie McQueen's *The Magic Bookshelf* and
10-year Anniversary Edition, *The New Magic Bookshelf:
Finding Great Books Your Child Will Treasure Forever*

"Finding the right book for one's child is absolutely essential for promoting a lifelong love of reading. *The New Magic Bookshelf: Finding Great Books Your Child Will Treasure Forever* is a guide for parents and educators in matching children with the right books that will spark that love for literacy, and teach them that reading can be as fun as any toy or video game... *The New Magic Bookshelf* is a solid acquisition for anyone seeking to promote literacy in their own or others' children."—*Midwest Book Review*

"Adults often forget the strong connection between these two skills [reading and writing]. One naturally leads to the other. And parents and guardians can do more than they might think to encourage the reading-writing link."—*Los Angeles Times Book Review*

"An outstanding resource for parents, teachers and others who care about the reading life of a child. The suggestions are practical, easily carried out, and inexpensive. The book lists are more useful than any I've seen, because they are designed to help parents get started on their personal program. You may be surprised at the books for children that are good literature... or you may just be surprised at how truly captivating children's books can be."—*Bella Online*

"The writing is clear and lucid, the concepts embrace a wide range of relevant and practical thinking, and all the content is driven by an appreciation and love of reading. The book is filled with original ideas." Robert McCarty, author of the *Planet of the Dogs* series and Academy Award nominee for the short film *Rooftops of New York*

"The advice that parents used to receive from teachers is that it doesn't matter what your child reads, just that she or he reads. This outstanding book takes appropriate issue with that way of thinking and proposes an alternative approach that will enrich your child's (or grandchild's) reading skills, knowledge of good stories, and ability to write."—*Amazon.com Top 100 reviewer*

"The [book] includes a wealth of information. I would heartily recommend it if you are looking to lure your children into literary enchantment."—*Heart of the Matter online*

HANGING ON BY MY FINGERNAILS

SURVIVING THE NEW DIVORCE GAMESMANSHIP, AND HOW A SCRATCH CAN LAND YOU IN JAIL

Janie McQueen

with legal commentary from Randall M. Kessler, Esq.
Kessler & Solomiany, LLC

Foreword by Tamara N. Holder

BURNING SAGE
ATLANTA

ISBN-13: 978-0981611402

LCCN: 2011933240

Publisher's Cataloging-in-Publication
(Provided by Quality Books, Inc.)
McQueen, Janie.
Hanging On By My Fingernails / Janie McQueen.
p. cm.
Includes bibliographical references and index.
LCCN 2011933240
ISBN-13: 978-0981611402
ISBN-10: 0981611400
ISBN-13: 978-0981611419
ISBN-10: 0981611419
[etc.]

1. Women prisoners--United States. 2. Criminal justice, Administration of-United States. I. Kessler, Randall M., 1962- II. Title.

HV8738.T73 2011
365'.6'0820973
QBI11-600134

EDITORIAL NOTES

The sources interviewed for this book appear with their permission, providing general input from their own areas of expertise, and do not necessarily share the author's or any other sources' points of view. Their insights are not meant to take the place of professional counsel, and indeed are not legal advice, but are shared to help the reader understand these complex issues. The only legal advice given is to hire a lawyer of one's own choosing to answer questions related to one's particular situation.

Likewise, the author is a journalist who has witnessed many of these practices firsthand, but she is not a legal professional or other authority. The suggestions and scenarios that appear here are for informational purposes so readers may make their own conclusions and choices. Other than sources' quotes and attributions, the opinions here are the author's own. This book should not serve as a substitute for advice from appropriate professionals.

The narratives in this book are presented in the words of the women and men who experienced them. Names and some identifying information have been changed to protect their identities. In several narratives, state of residence has been omitted but the arrest policy of that state is given. All sources quoted in this book are real, and come from all parts of the United States.

CONTENTS

FOREWORD

An abusive man never stops crafting unique ways to hurt the woman he claims he loves.

There is no rulebook that says: "You are not a victim of domestic abuse unless you have bruises around your neck, a bloody nose, or a bump on the back of your head." That's why the most adept abuser is constantly designing different tools to add to his war chest, many of which do not leave a single physical wound.

The most recent statistics reveal *three* women a day lose their lives at the hands of their intimate partners.

Aasiya Zubair was one of these women who make up the statistic. In 2009, she filed for divorce from her husband, Muzzammil Syed Hassan. Prior to her filing, police had visited the couple's home many times, in response to her 9-1-1 calls about his abuse.

Despite Aasiya's 21-page affidavit detailing numerous instances of Hassan's torture and abuse, he was never prosecuted. On the very day she served him the divorce papers, he brutally killed her, stabbing her over 40 times and then beheading her.

Hassan did not deny the murder; instead, he claimed he acted in self-defense and she was the abuser. (Hassan even went so far as to write local newspapers, claiming he was a "POW" and "slave" to Aasiya's abuse.)

What about the women who are not murdered by their husbands or boyfriends? If three women per day are killed as a result of domestic abuse, how many live day to day with abuse?

Fortunately, in recent years, more opportunities for women to seek help have been created: a more efficient 9-1-1 system, domestic abuse laws, women's shelters... Some states offer a "no notice" order of protection, in which a judge enters a short-term restraining order against an abuser without the abuser knowing of the order. It it's violated, even though he didn't know about it, he'll be arrested.

This book exposes how men manipulate the single thing abused women thought they now had on their side: the criminal justice system.

Unfortunately, many abusive men have learned to reshape domestic violence laws into another weapon of abuse. They are turning police and court protections upside down: The abusers themselves call 9-1-1; they have the woman arrested for domestic violence; and then they do everything they can to try to have the woman prosecuted and sentenced. In this way, the true victim is painted as the abuser.

There's a deeper motivation in using this ploy: to show a pattern of "violent conduct" on the woman's part so that the abuser can use it as evidence against her in a divorce or child custody battle. And this form of abuse is permanent. A bruise heals after a few days, but a conviction for a violent crime mars her record forever.

The set-up: A couple has a fight. Either the wife calls 9-1-1 in a desperate plea for police intervention, or the husband makes the call first in a preemptive attack. When the police arrive, the woman is visibly upset. The man, on the other hand, is extremely calm as he switches off his anger. The husband tells the police that his wife is delusional, crazy, and violent. Depending on how convincing the man's story is to the police officer, and the state's law on domestic violence, either both people are arrested or the woman is arrested.

In the case of dual arrest, which some states discourage, the woman often tells prosecutors she doesn't want to testify against her husband, so the case is dismissed. Meanwhile, the husband is determined that she be prosecuted. Instead of the prosecutors looking into the history of the relationship before proceeding with the criminal case, they move full speed ahead. The wife is usually cut off from her husband's financial support so she cannot pay for defense against him. As a result, she is forced to take a plea to the charges because she cannot afford to defend herself. She fears taking the case to trial, losing, and going to jail.

In most states, violent crimes—especially those involving domestic abuse—permanently remain on one's record. Some states (like Illinois, where I practice) have expungement laws; however, this remedy is only available to the person who was *not convicted*. A person convicted of a violent crime must generally seek a Governor's pardon. A pardon is rare, and the violent offender is usually the least likely to receive such a remedy. *At least a bruise heals over time; a conviction is forever*. What company wants to hire a woman with a violent crime on her background?

For the first time ever, this new form of abuse is exposed: the abused woman whose husband or boyfriend tells police and courts that he is the victim.

This is Aasiya's story; unfortunately, she cannot share it herself because she was permanently silenced.

The legal manipulations comprise Janie McQueen's story. This could also be your friend's story. Or maybe it's *your* story.

To the women who are victims of domestic abuse or "divorce gamesmanship": Look no further. This book will give you hope and courage, and most of all, real tools to break free.

To prosecutors, police and attorneys: It is time to expand your awareness and realize that this type of abuse is becoming more prevalent. Each man's allegation of spousal abuse must be fully investigated before the woman is prosecuted.

To friends and family: Look beyond a bruise for signs of domestic abuse of a loved one.

We can no longer wait for the next woman to be exposed to this newly evolved form of abuse and torture. We can no longer remain silent.

My grandfather Frank Holder always told me, "No fear." As you read this book, I pass his words on to you.

No fear. Protect yourself and defend yourself against any kind of abuse, even if it doesn't leave a mark or a bruise. *No fear.*

Tamara N. Holder
Chicago, Illinois
May 2, 2011
www.theholderposition.com

꙰

"No single event can awaken within us a stranger whose existence we had never suspected. To live is to be slowly born."
—Antoine de Saint-Exupéry, Flight to Arras

PROLOGUE

Set-Up
Suburban Atlanta, April 2007
Friday, 9:30 p.m.

P eter held his cell phone high, well out of my reach, randomly
punching in numbers. He was threatening to call my boss at the
fitness center—granted, not the most important, career-
building job in the world, but it was my job, even if it was part-time.
Looking back, I do not know what he proposed to tell my boss—he just
said he was calling "to tell her about me." Obviously, I cared enough to
try to stop him. His clear implication was he was seeking to defame my
character or otherwise embarrass me in some way. He was not calling her
to discuss my talent for Parent-Tot Water Fun. Later I realized Peter
probably had no real numbers to call. My carefully constructed outside
life was so fragile and inordinately important by then, I took the bait.

Peter continued to pound numbers and taunt me. Terrified of being humiliated to my boss, I jumped for the phone, my 5'5", 120 pounds to his 5'9", 240. This continued for about 15 minutes or so, until we were fighting in earnest for possession of the phone. At one point, we tumbled down the stairs, where I collapsed in a heap at the bottom, banged up from shins to collarbone. Peter got up but instead of helping me, as I actually expected, he continued with the implied threats. Our little boys were asleep in their rooms upstairs, and, mercifully, did not wake. No one was yelling. It was an oddly quiet, purely physical struggle, the first marital argument to morph into anything like this.

Gradually the taunts of calling my boss switched to threats of calling the police. By now the fighting had subsided. I was on my knees, rocking back on my heels, begging him not to call. "Please don't do this. One of us should just leave, take a break. It's not worth it." I distinctly remember the moment Peter completed that call. By this time, we had stopped fighting altogether and I just sat staring at him, astonished. He seemed composed, smug. Then he gasped into the phone: "NEED HELP!"

"Are you really going to do this?" I asked, still not believing.

Georgia is not a mandatory arrest state. This means that if the police are summoned to an incident of alleged domestic violence, they are not required to arrest someone. Yet, the officer in charge told me more than once: "We get a call, someone's going in."

The police arrived quickly. Peter let them in. He remained in the entrance hall. Two male officers pushed me back into the master bedroom so they could interview us individually. I recounted my side of the story, just stating we had a fight; we were both a little bruised up from an argument over the phone; and that I thought it was now under control. The questions and my answers went something like this: "He said you are having an affair." "What? Of course not, I guess I rather thought he was." "Did you scratch him?" "I guess I might have by accident. I was trying to get the phone. But I have bruises too, see?" "Did you try to stop him from calling 9-1-1?" "Yes, I thought we could solve this on our own." I did not include the part about his taunting me with the phone. I still thought we could tell them to go away; it would be all right. Things got out of hand, but we could manage. Divorce was imminent, but I did not think to say so. Nobody asked anyway.

The officer interrogating me turned to his co-officers and called, "We've got probable cause."

He turned back to me. "You are under arrest for criminal domestic violence," he said. "One count of simple battery, and one count of interference with a 9-1-1 call."

I later cringed to learn that if my sons had been awake, I also could have been charged with cruelty to children. Such a charge would have broken my heart. I am not sure how I would have dealt with the emotional fallout. Just the basic domestic violence charges were a significant burden.

The police officers handcuffed me and led me out of my house, in my Friday night at home attire of tie-dyed T-shirt, jeans, and bare feet. Suddenly aware I was apparently being made responsible for the events of the entire evening, I tried again to get them to record my bruises. They ignored me. Peter had collapsed by the stairs. "I didn't want this!" he cried.

"What is happening?" I hissed.

1

WHAT IS HAPPENING?

"A question that sometimes drives me hazy: Am I or the others crazy?"
—Albert Einstein

Handcuffed and seated in the back of a police car, blue lights flashing, is not where most people expect to be at 10:30 on Friday night, or any other night. I was no different. I was in that suspended state of disbelief you have when something extraordinary, or horrible, is happening. The trip was surreal. We glided down the eerily peaceful, dark streets of the town. I recognized our route. We were heading in the direction of the main library branch, where the boys and I attended 95 percent of the free programming, past the cultural arts center where I had subjected them to the ballet more than once.

We finally came to a stop just around the corner, at the police department. Behind it was the detention center. I marveled at how vastly different were the functions of buildings that shared space in this corner of the city.

Police stations were rather ordinary to me. I am a career journalist and have worked the cop beat for two major metropolitan newspapers. Stopping by police departments and detention centers for records and news morsels was routine.

Normalcy ended there. I was booked and spent that Friday night alone in a holding cell staring at the only reading material available: a word of graffiti on the ceiling. *Satan.*

All night I listened to the drunken wailing of the rest of the Friday night posse with nothing to do but read that word, repeatedly. The more I looked at it, the more terrified I became. It seemed like a signature. "This visit to hell was brought to you by: *Satan.*"

I was still barefoot and beginning to regret my refusal of the ugly beige PVC plastic prison sandals. But I was certain someone would detect the Big Mistake at any moment, and I could go home. I knew I was going to be a no-show at work the next day—Saturday was big swim lesson day—and I wanted things to be normal. Quick. Mostly I worried about my children waking the next morning and finding me gone. How long would I be in here? Who would take care of them?

When they finally let me out of the holding cell the next morning, I was exhausted. A guard led me to a larger area with a shower, and told me to remove my clothes. Then he stepped away. I was stunned. The female guard armed with a big bottle of delousing liquid must have noted that. "Why do I need to do this when I'm leaving?" I asked.

"You're not leaving," she answered, not unkindly. "You're being admitted."

No one had caught the Big Mistake after all.

In the beginning, I struggled to understand how a part-time swim instructor and average suburban mom landed in jail after a marital argument I did not start, and which left me with significantly worse physical injuries than the 9-1-1 caller. Admittedly, it was an awful fight. One moment all was its usual uncomfortable, strained pre-divorce atmosphere in the home; and the next, the match was struck and Peter and I were fighting over the cell phone. But if both of us were equally to blame, why did they only arrest me?

At first I still did not see the connection between increasingly odd behavior going on in the house and the 9-1-1 call. I regarded my arrest as an isolated incident. It seemed wrong and grossly unfair, not to mention humiliating and nearly soul-crushing at the time, but I had my hands full fighting a divorce war that centered on a full-blown custody battle the moment I stepped out of the detention center.

However, not long after my arrest, I was shocked to hear about two other women in my community who had not been as "fortunate" as I was, just to go to the local detention center after 9-1-1 calls made by their husbands. That was distressing enough. These two did their couple of days at the boisterous metropolitan city jail, a far scarier institution. One of the women was an art dealer, the other a nursery school director. So now I knew I had company. I still had no idea a larger issue might be at the root of our arrests.

Then I met a third connection, one much closer to home. One afternoon at the fitness center, I ran into a college friend, Jessica, whom I had not seen in 20 years. Amazingly, she happened to be living in the same Georgia suburb as I, even though neither of us had prior ties there.

In a phone conversation several weeks later, as Jessica described her divorce several years earlier, out tumbled the same arrest and jail story, ending in the same jail. I was stunned. It was uncanny.

After this revelation, we often discussed the similarities of our experiences, but we just couldn't wrap our arms around them. "Is this happening?" we asked ourselves over and over.

So I put myself on the crime beat again. With Jessica's help, I began to gather information, talking with other women, domestic violence experts, lawyers, and police. I realized that although the chance meeting with my college friend was an extraordinary coincidence, the shared experience was not so rare. Was this happening? Are police officers arresting women and taking them to jail so often for arguably unnecessary calls made by their husbands? I was surprised but gratified I was not imagining things when I heard a resounding "yes."

"It's a very, very common practice," domestic violence expert Lundy Bancroft, author of *Why Does He Do That? Inside the Minds of Angry and Controlling Men,* affirmed to me. "It does seem like arranging to have the woman arrested is increasing, or at least it's staying very common among abusers."

The phenomenon of women being arrested more frequently than before as the primary aggressor in domestic violence disputes also is happening in other parts of the world. A study on domestic abuse and gender, conducted by Bristol University in England, found women are three times more likely to be arrested in domestic violence incidents as men. The "vast majority" of perpetrators of domestic violence are men, the study found; yet women are arrested in three of every ten incidents, and men in only one of ten.[1]

I recently sat next to a fit, 60-ish woman at a local barbecue joint as we waited for takeout orders. When she told me that she operated a bail bonding agency, I told her about this book. I asked her if she noticed this trend. "Oh yes," she said.

"So who seems to be arrested more—men or women?" I pressed. "Women," she said emphatically. "I see a lot of unnecessary arrests."

Since I began studying this seeming anomaly, many women who have found themselves on the wrong side of a 9-1-1 call have emerged from behind this curtain of humiliation; they are sorry this happened to others, but relieved they have company. This is not something women are likely to disclose to others. They suffer from the dehumanizing experience and a litany of other problems economic to social, often alone.

"If it proves to be tricky and difficult to remove this arrest from my record, then that will just be further evidence of how victimizing the arrest laws are," said Ashley, 40, whose husband, a big player in their metro area news industry, recently called 9-1-1 to "report" her. Ashley had attempted to get in between a scuffle between him and their 11-year-old son, and her husband retaliated. They live in a Midwestern state where the law provides that when police respond to a domestic violence call, they can make an arrest at the police officers' discretion.

---

[1] Hester, M. *Who Does What to Whom? Gender and Domestic Violence Perpetrators.* (2009) Bristol: University of Bristol in association with the Northern Rock Foundation.

However, the police at the scene were forced by their supervisor to make an arrest, she said. "As if the handcuffing at the curb of my street, the booking process, the time in the jail cell, the trauma to the children, the threat of being kept away from home for three days—had he not agreed to waive the accompanying restraining order—and the difficulty keeping this private... weren't already enough."

Because of her arrest, Ashley was a no-show the next day at work as a church business manager, setting tongues wagging. The local newspaper published her arrest in the blotter, adding to her embarrassment. "All the while, in addition to the time this takes up, legal services and counseling cost money," she added. "We're nearly bankrupt from medical expenses." Her younger son suffers from leukemia.

Reducing this complicated matter to its simplest terms, dialing 9-1-1 on one's spouse and arranging to have him or her arrested has become what many attorneys shrug off as part of the current "divorce gamesmanship." Indeed, a common mantra in the divorce tactical arena is, "Get to the phone first."[2]

By all accounts the 9-1-1 caller, if the police know who it is, has the distinct advantage. He or she is the 9-1-1 host, as it were. In this way the caller, whether male or female, can manipulate the investigation and try to capture the empathy of the police. The "game" is to get a leg up in the divorce by making the partner look incompetent and distract him or her with trying to clear her name, while the real perpetrator gets down to business setting up the rest of the divorce proceedings.

---

[2] Crager, Meg; Cousin, Merril; Hardy, Tara. *Victim-Defendants: An Emerging Challenge in Responding to Domestic Violence in Seattle and the King County Region (April 2003).* King County Coalition Against Domestic Violence, reprinted by the Minnesota Center Against Violence and Abuse. Web. 5 June 2011.

Websites such as *www.dumpyourwifenow.com* and others geared toward the "fathers' rights" movement offer additional creative weapons for the divorce war, ranging from "prepare to treat her as your mortal enemy" to "change the locks and notify your attorney that you want a restraining order."[3] Web searches yield these sites abound. Lawyers seeking to capture the often fatter male wallet appear to run many of these websites. I found few female-oriented sites that are so outwardly hostile.

Falling in the Margins

A related version of this same game came up last year in the news, when former Arizona state senator Scott Bundgaard used the "legislative immunity" excuse to avoid arrest after a fight with his then girlfriend, Aubry Ballard. Evidence showed the two had a physical argument, and both showed mild injuries, but because Bundgaard cited an obscure law, Ballard alone went to jail. Bundgaard was later charged with reckless endangerment and assault. Ballard was required to testify at a live Senate Ethics Hearing, along with the other four witnesses to the fight. The next day, just before he was to testify, Bundgaard resigned from his Senate position.

This tactic is despicable no matter who employs it. This book does not intend to male bash, but rather to show the female point of view, which I and many of my sources feel is under reported. I also do not seek to slam the system or particular agencies, but to show that they are not functioning well as a whole.

---

[3] "Divorce Self Defense 101". *www.dumpyourwifenow.com*. Dump Your Wife Now! 2008-2011. Web. 16 February 2012.

I was dismayed but ultimately unsurprised that some bureaucratic types I reached out to in the research phase expressed sympathy but mostly treated the victims as statistics—unfortunates who got caught between a policy that was intended to do good, and a police force interpreting these stiff policies on their own. Indeed, one federally funded domestic violence research institution I contacted downplayed these experiences and felt I was being overly critical of the laws. "We are your allies," the director told me, "not your opponents."

He appeared interested in my manuscript and gave me constructive criticisms; some suggestions were genuinely helpful and others seemed to be merely defensive of policy. He suggested more criticism should be aimed at the "poorly trained local police." I pointed out that the government agency he was defending is authorized to allocate millions of dollars per year for police training. (The total budget for federal programs relating to domestic violence for 2011 was $730 million.)[4] In the end, the agency refused to go on record with any supporting information or insights and even declined a mention in my acknowledgments. In sum, they claimed a polite but arm's-length desire to help but seemed to really want nothing to do with me or the women I was writing about.

Although I uncovered extensive research documenting this trend in scholarly journals, I found nothing in the public domain for women like us. Our stories and preliminary research even shocked my closest friends. "I had no idea this was happening!" was the standard,

---

[4] "The White House's Commitment to Combating Violence Against Women."
The White House. N.p., n.d. Web. 7 March 2012.
www.whitehouse.gov/sites/default/files/20100202-whitehouse-combating-violence-against-women.pdf

incredulous refrain. Some friends called back a week or two later saying, "You'll never believe that a friend of mine said she was going through the very same thing!"

Unfortunately, I believed it.

One male respondent to my request for sources brought up his own evidence that women resort to this ploy, as well. "From personal experience, I know this drill," said Steven, a computer technician. "I filed for divorce. For the next six years, my wife made horrible accusations. When I got to court, there was no real trial, no evidence, just a judge being afraid to trust that the accusations might possibly be false, not asking for any proof, and not wanting to be anything but politically correct." Steven's story appears later in this book; he seems a dedicated father with a very vindictive ex-wife. This book does not suggest women do not use this ploy, nor that mothers are always better parents than fathers.

Extreme fathers' rights groups in particular have touted the male experience, and scholarly journals and federally funded state studies have explored the paradox of domestic violence victims as arrestees for years. (A sampling of these can be found in Appendix C.) However, as of this writing, I had not seen anything in the popular press noting this significant backlash effect, in which the 9-1-1 caller might well be the perpetrator himself. I also have not seen anything in scholarly journals about what happens to the women who are arrested.

There are many angles, from cautionary and educational, to societal and legal, from which to report this phenomenon. This book aims to look at the problem from as many sides as possible, but its primary goal is to help educate women and shout out loud that *it is happening.*

Beyond Booking

A few attorneys I spoke with—not those cited in this book—minimized these experiences, saying, "Well, you do your couple of days and then you get out." As prominent divorce attorney Randy Kessler pointed out, you must focus on that end goal, to try to clear your record and secure a solid future for yourself and your children, if you have them. It is, of course, not the worst thing that can happen.

But even Kessler, from the comfort of his penthouse office in downtown Atlanta, well understands the ploy's lingering effects. My initial cold call to Kessler's office yielded an affirmative response, an "oh yes" that this was happening, so frequently, in fact, that it was almost old news to the attorneys who have to pick up the pieces on a daily basis. But the ploy's long-term destructive effects are evident in how hard it is for some victims to even gather the courage to leave a bad relationship, Kessler said.

This is one reason this experience is so complicated and difficult; it is very hard for a woman to "be strong and fight" when she is afraid, her self esteem is demolished, and she is being treated like a criminal. Getting in fight mode requires steely strength. That's why I have put the jail experience at the core—but it fans out to many other issues.

The experience brings with it staggering financial burdens on the woman and the emotional taxation of enduring her own criminal trial, if it comes to that, before she can proceed with a divorce, which is emotionally depleting in itself. Some particularly vindictive partners compound the financial strain with "paper abuse," a sort of bullying via legal maneuvers that ties up the victim and the court system with frivolous lawsuits and more false charges that further suck up already limited resources.[5]

So I quickly realized the *what* in the equation. I knew from experience what happens to the woman when she gets out of jail. There is not only a broken marriage, an ugly divorce, and often a traumatic custody battle. She starts out at a severe disadvantage because of the charges alone (even if they can be dropped). Particularly if she has been a stay-at-home mom, she probably does not have access to the financial resources her husband does.

Often charges and court stipulations that follow an arrest—like automatic restraining orders—at least temporarily separate her from her children and cast her in the light of an unfit mother. The sight of their mother led away in handcuffs terrorizes her children if they are present. The local police blotter informs the community, and children who catch wind of it tease the children involved because their daddy sent their mommy to jail. The whispering of former friends alienates and humiliates the woman who takes the fall for misapplications of mandatory arrest, pro-arrest, and even discretionary arrest laws. Her spouse lords it over her for the remainder of the marriage, and uses it to gain an unfair advantage in the ensuing divorce and custody trials.

With the criminal domestic violence charge against her (and a child cruelty charge to boot, if her children were present during the

---

[5] Miller, Susan L., and Nicole L. Smolter. "'Paper Abuse'": When All Else Fails, Batterers Use Procedural Stalking." *Violence Against Women*. Sage Publications, 28 Apr. 2011. Web. 24 June 2011.

arrest), a woman may have little support when she declares even rightfully that she is a good mother.

For me, I found some peoples' questioning whether or not I was a good mother the hardest, most heartbreaking part of the experience.

So I was beginning to get an idea of the *what* and the *who* concerning these arrests. Next I was determined to find out exactly *how* and, most of all, *why.*

Domestic Violence Defined

The U. S. Office on Violence Against Women (OVW) defines domestic violence as "a pattern of abusive behavior in any relationship that is used by one partner to gain or maintain power and control over another intimate partner." Domestic violence can happen to anyone regardless of age, gender, race, sexual orientation, or religion. Domestic violence can be physical, sexual, emotional, economic, or psychological actions or threats of actions that affect another person. This includes any behaviors that "intimidate, manipulate, humiliate, isolate, frighten, terrorize, coerce, threaten, blame, hurt, injure, or wound someone."

Domestic violence is not only an issue for married couples, but also those who are living together or dating. Domestic violence affects people of all socioeconomic backgrounds and education levels.

Source: "USDOJ: Office on Violence Against Women: Crimes of Focus: Domestic Violence." N.p., n.d. Web. 24 June 2011. *www.ovw.usdoj.gov/domviolence.htm*

2

"SOMEONE'S GOING IN"

"Tis much more prudence to acquit two persons, though actually guilty, than to pass sentence of condemnation on one that is virtuous and innocent."
—Voltaire

Researchers and domestic violence experts throughout the country have recognized the increasing arrests of females for domestic violence, theorizing they may stem from a complex combination of causes.[6] The problem of domestic violence, which had laid squarely in the social issue area, moved into the criminal domain with a sequence of laws, most notably the formulation of the Violence Against Women Act in 1994.[7] This act led to local adoptions of mandatory arrest

---

[6] DeSantis, Marie. "Advocating for Domestic Violence Victims Who Have Been Arrested for Domestic Violence." Web. 6 June 2011.
http://justicewomen.com/tips_dv_victims.html

[7] "Violence Against Women Act (VAWA) National Domestic Violence Hotline: 10 Years of Progress and Moving Forward." N.p., n.d. Web. 24 June 2011.
http://www.thehotline.org/get-educated/violence-against-women-act-vawa/

and other rigid pro-arrest policies, which are examined in detail later in this book. (Mandatory arrest laws gained popularity after the Minneapolis Domestic Violence Experiment, a landmark 1982 study that claimed arrest is a more effective means of preventing domestic violence than separating the partners or trying to talk through the problem.[8])

Steve Kardian, a retired New York police officer who now runs a women's self defense program and lectures widely on safety issues, believes the clamping down on arrests hit full stride with the O.J. Simpson trial in the 1990s. During the highly publicized trial of the former pro football player and media celebrity for the alleged murder of his ex-wife, prosecutors noted that police repeatedly refused to arrest and charge Simpson when Nicole Brown Simpson had called for police assistance. "Ever since O.J., the onus has been put onto law enforcement," Kardian said. "That was the huge turning point."

There also sometimes seems to be a blurring of lines between "mandatory arrest" and "discretionary arrest." Georgia is technically an "officer discretionary arrest" state, but the arresting officers told both Jessica and me, "We get a domestic violence call, someone's going in." The official Georgia law might not show it, but it sure sounded like mandatory arrest to us. When I contacted the local police department that conducted our arrests, the officer who responded denied someone had to go in every time. He admitted sometimes they get it wrong; but that there is also a natural bias toward the caller if the caller is identified. "It's perceived they needed help, obviously," he said.

---

[8] Sherman, Lawrence W., and Richard A. Berk. "The Minneapolis Domestic Violence Experiment." *Police Foundation Reports* May (1984): 1. Print.

This was a young officer, and perhaps the department has altered its arrest practices since our arrests. Their approach might also have to do with the mindset of the leading investigative officer, and the supervisor on duty, as in Ashley's case. It is not a science, which is why the issue of domestic violence issues resting in the hands of law enforcement is murky.

Filtering Facts

Police departments typically do not keep records of 9-1-1 callers. 9-1-1 is an autonomous system; police often do not have this information when they go out to investigate.

"Most responding officers do not hear the caller when they call for service," agreed Jeffrey Smallwood, a former Deputy Sheriff with the Orange County Sheriff's Office in Orlando, Florida, who specialized in in-service education and policy review for the police academy. "When we arrive, we may be met by the caller or not. Most of the time, I never asked 'who' called. Instead, I asked, 'Did you call?' only if I had the luxury of the introduction. Many times you arrive in a heated verbal exchange and you wade into the swamp, so to speak, and separate parties and start listening or asking questions."

Smallwood and other law enforcement officers I interviewed vehemently denied gender bias in police training. They allowed mistakes happen, but the police receive training on how to weed out the aggressor; to transport the victim for help if needed; and to keep the peace. Their strategy is to go first to the caller, if known, and then separate the parties to get clear stories. Obviously, the fates of the respondees rely on the degree of training and the officers' innate senses of human nature and

15

intuition, which is difficult if not impossible to instill. A staggering amount of power and discretion in carrying out these stringent laws rests on their shoulders even as they have limited knowledge and time.

Marie DeSantis of the Women's Justice Center based in Santa Rosa, California runs a website devoted to improving outcomes for women and information on how to support domestic violence victims who are themselves arrested for domestic violence. She believes police officers too often fail to properly identify the dominant aggressor. "In a common variation of this problem, the officer fails to correctly identify defensive wounds and, as a result, they are arresting women who defend themselves, especially those women who defend themselves successfully," she reports. "And in another whole set of cases, there are indications that domestic violence perpetrators themselves have gotten increasingly sophisticated at turning the law on women by doing such things as calling 9-1-1 themselves or by purposely injuring themselves before police arrive."[9] Officers need to check to make sure the injuries match the stories, she stresses.

Obviously, there are instances in which the arrest of females for domestic violence is legitimate. But the women represented in this book have their own eyewitness accounts to add to expert confirmations that there are too many cases in which the woman is bruised black and blue, yet she is arrested because the man has a bleeding scratch on his face or chest.

Jessica had operated more or less in a daze after her arrest. Though she filed for divorce immediately after her parents picked her up

---

[9] Marie DeSantis, *www.justicewomen.com*

from the detention center, she did not pursue it and remained married for one more year. She had forgotten if she had even seen her own police report before discovering a copy of it years later.

Sandy-haired, blue-eyed Jessica was shocked as she studied the description of herself in the incident report: brown eyes and black hair. These were not her physical attributes, obviously. They were those of her husband. We realized that, whether out of careless, hasty error, a rote response system, or, worse, an unconcern about what happened, the responding officers must have written the report on the spot, on her husband's testimony alone. In other words, the police had reached their conclusion well before they caught up to Jessica on her friend's front lawn. Indeed, from their report, it would seem they never even looked at her.

All through this sorting-out process, Jessica and I had been trying to make sense of our bewildering experiences—if we were solely at fault, to figure out why—and sincerely tried to hold on to a non-cynical viewpoint. Instead, we became statistics. Our families' very futures appeared to hinge on well intentioned but aggressive laws. A complex incident reporting system does not require police departments to identify the caller or submit complete reports, including who is arrested. Though both Jessica and I came to realize we might have handled our situations in ways that may have kept them from escalating, it was beginning to seem that grant money, if unintentionally, literally rewarded arrests, including ours.

Poisoning the Well

Bonnie Russell, who founded *www.familylawcourts.com* in 2001 after growing increasingly dissatisfied with media coverage of family courts in San Diego, contends men often call the police "for the express purpose of poisoning the well."

"They use red flag phrases such as 'She's emotionally unstable,' or to typecast, 'She goes crazy during certain times of the month,'" Russell said. "However, the really crafty say, 'I'm afraid of her.' This immediately makes the police—including female officers—act to protect the guy who just set them up."

Jessica's shockingly inaccurate incident report seems to confirm this. All her husband apparently had to do was tell the police that she was out of control, had been drinking a little wine, and show that scratch.

Tamara Holder, a Chicago-based criminal defense attorney who specializes in helping victims expunge their records, a tricky process in Illinois, agrees, adding these isolated incidents extend far deeper. "Women who are the victims of this tactic are often victims of other abuse from the spouse," she said. "This is just another 'f**k you' tactic. These men are master manipulators. These are battered women—they don't need bruises to be battered—and the men do this because they know they can."

Mandatory Versus Discretionary Arrest

Domestic violence arrest laws currently require police to arrest the alleged attacker regardless of the victim's wishes. These laws replace older policies in which the victim could decide not to press charges and thus prohibit an arrest. These laws put the police squarely in charge.

"Police have got to get there and make sure if it's a domestic violence case, that we can't leave unless we've ensured both parties are safe," safety expert Steve Kardian said. "What's good about the system today is that if the police officer feels in any way, shape or form that there is any danger," he or she can take action without the victim's consent.

Many states have adopted mandatory arrest policies, in which if the police receive a 9-1-1 domestic violence call, an arrest must be made. "Preferred arrest" states encourage arrests but are less strict that mandatory arrest laws.[10]

Discretionary arrest means just that—officers are authorized to make an arrest if they determine a primary aggressor. The policies were devised to protect victims by removing them from immediate danger (so nothing worse would happen), and forcing police to act. These laws, though pushed farther by legislation such as VAWA, are rooted in the

---

[10] Hirschel, David. "Domestic Violence Cases: What Research Shows About Arrest and Dual Arrest Rates." *National Institute of Justice: Criminal Justice Research, Development and Evaluation.* N.p., 25 July 2008. Web. 24 June 2011. *http://www.nij.gov/publications/dv-dual-arrest-222679/welcome.htm*

Minneapolis Domestic Violence Experiment, which determined this was a more effective approach than the traditional actions of separating the couple for a few hours or trying to talk them through the problem.[11]

Based on the premise that victims of abuse are too fearful to speak up, the police act on their behalf, and take responsibility for the arrest (just like what both Jessica and I were told in our arrests, although Georgia is not a mandatory arrest state).

According to the U.S. Department of Justice, 22 states and the District of Columbia had adopted mandatory arrest laws as of September 2009. The laws are constantly changing, and vary from state to state as to whether the incident meets conditions requiring arrest. These include the nature of the relationship of the people involved; whether there was a serious injury that could result in death; whether the couple has a child together; and so on. For a breakdown of arrest polices by state, see Appendix A.

---

[11] Sherman and Beck. "The Minneapolis Domestic Violence Experiment." 1.

3
CLUB 9-1-1

"Prison's not a nice place to be. Those people are not in there for singing in the choir."
—Larry Todd, former spokesman for the Texas Department of Criminal Justice

O vernight Peter brought my antidepressant meds to the detention center. I was still in the holding cell and was let out only briefly to first retrieve my meds, then hand them over to the guards. Peter seemed rattled and confused, perhaps as shocked as I was. Maybe a little guilty. Through the whole experience, however, he seemed determined to justify why it was I who deserved to be behind bars.

The prison was teeming. I think it was a full moon night. It was the kind of night we called a "good story night" back when I was on the police desk, a night full of juicy tidbits for tomorrow's paper.

I did not expect to one day be among the Friday night arrest records I used to eagerly rifle through.

Now clad in a prison-issue orange jumpsuit and slippery acrylic socks, I was ushered up to the large common area of the detention center allocated for females. Women of diverse descriptions were sitting around, watching TV, talking, or staring listlessly out of the barred windows. I had covered a couple of Scared Straight programs and attended the openings of various deluxe modern detention centers in tiny towns, but it was a shocking moment to realize I was the one being committed here.

Here, as a real, if temporary, resident, I saw mostly lethargy and apathy. To be sure, there were threatening overtones by the mere nature of it, and I was extremely intimidated. I worried someone would beat me up. A couple of heated phone calls home in which I demanded to be released during my stay upped my social standing a little. "She's really giving him what for," I heard one inmate say approvingly. "You go girl."

It was becoming apparent with every phone call home—I slid to the communal phone as often as possible—that Peter was becoming more and more "coached." The initial shock and dismay, even if feigned, was unmistakably hardening into calculation. At one point, he mentioned my wine drinking, which I considered moderate, and which had never been an issue in the marriage. Peter was a teetotaler, which I learned can work in one's favor if one chooses to be self righteous about it.

(Alcohol use is an easy target and frequently used. Most men who put my female sources in jail were quick to cite "alcohol abuse." None of the women I interviewed seemed to be heavy drinkers. I later proved I am a card-carrying non alcoholic after consulting a highly regarded addictions expert as part of my expensive defense.)

By this time, it was becoming apparent Peter was talking to people, many people. He had gone with both of our boys to the home of some then-friends. He had acquired an attorney. My mother told me that when she accused him of setting me up he protested, "I'm trying not to!"

Eventually I met my cellmate, Vanessa. She was hardened; probably in her mid to late 40s. But she was empathetic, especially considering she was being obliged to share her precious single cell with me now. The prison was that full. My bed was a thin mattress on the floor with a flimsy pillow and a threadbare cotton blanket.

Vanessa clearly had prominence in the invisible social structure of the place. This was a city jail, a detention center, but inmates could be detained there for up to a year. Vanessa seemed to have served at least a combined 364 days through various jail stints she recounted.

She showed me the ropes. The skills I learned included, but were not limited to, pocketing extra cookies at mealtime; acting detached when the cell mate used the toilet; and most useful of all, perfecting the art of pretending to be somewhere else. This all became more handy when our unit was put in lockdown because of an unruly inmate.

I am more than a little claustrophobic, and lockdown in a tiny single unit for about 20 hours almost undid me. But we passed time. Vanessa told me about her boyfriend. It became clear she had a history of poor selections in romantic partners. This boyfriend was into petty theft. I realized my taste in men up until then was perhaps just as poor. I was, after all, in the same place as Vanessa.

I shared a few yoga moves to help us stay calm as the walls closed in. (Even downward facing dog is a devilishly difficult pose for two people of average height sharing a tiny single cell.) I read a little *Good News for*

Modern Man. (In the "library," there was a variety of Bibles in English and Spanish, and little else.) I lay down on my mattress and closed my eyes to block out the ugly cinder block walls and the ubiquitous fluorescent light that was always on. I wished the place away, traveling in my mind to the coastal home of my late grandparents, where I spent much of my time as a child.

I pictured the expansive gardens of flowers and vegetables my chemistry professor grandfather planted and devotedly tended, and the large, airy rooms, wood floors, and high ceilings of their Antebellum house. I thought about the lunches my elegant, exceptionally practical grandmother prepared: chicken and rice; fresh tomatoes and cucumbers from the garden; thin, dense biscuits with butter; saucers of Waldorf salad; and saccharine-sweetened tea, with an aftertaste I can still summon.

Hungrier than ever now, I mentally conjured up my grandmother's long pans of "fudge squares," the house dessert, which could be found in the refrigerator on any given day and topped with Breyers vanilla bean ice cream. I thought about oyster roasts in months with an "R," of the long steaming tables of gray and white shells (which would be dumped into the driveway after they were all shucked); of visiting aunts and uncles wandering around with tinkling "grown-up" drinks in my grandfather's gold-etched highball glasses. We children would sit on the back screened porch already expertly peeling boiled shrimp and shucking oysters, drinking Fresca and RC cola drawn from a huge chest of ice. (These were fancy suppers; on an ordinary night, the children's meal might well be wooden bowls of steaming "hominy" [grits] laced with salt and butter. Formal "dinner," in the Southern way, was the mid-day meal.)

I would have traded all my precious cookies for a bowl of hominy right then.

I imagined away that hard little mattress and remembered how wonderful it felt to sink into the soft pillows on the antique sleigh bed in "my" bedroom upstairs and cover up with a sweet-smelling quilt, listening to the grown-ups and their relaxing party in the dark Carolina night.

I thought about my children and how they never got to go there.

This made me so sad, I even made Vanessa cry. So I made myself stop.

The next day, before the guards lifted the lockdown, they permitted us a break outside our cells if we wanted to write a letter. Well, I am a writer, but even if I had not wanted to write a letter, you could be jolly darn sure I would have written one anyway to get out for even a few minutes. I was amazed only I and one other inmate chose to write letters. I remember her handwriting, large loopy high-schoolish cursive. I wrote about my children in my illegible reporter's scrawl. I cried some more.

During our brief time together, my pen pal, as it were, shared that she was in for an incident that seemed to involve a cousin's boyfriend, whom she had caught cheating with another woman. Whatever she did to him in retaliation, she was additionally charged with cruelty to children because her cousin's children were present in the house.

At that point, I knew I had dodged a bullet. The kind that could have been deadly.

Sunday afternoon, the guards called on me. Lockdown was over, and we were all hanging around, perked up a little at being let out into the comparatively sunny, if dingy, common room. I thought I was getting out. The other inmates openly snickered at me when I wished them all a heartfelt goodbye and best wishes. "She thinks she's leaving!" one tittered.

The guards handcuffed me and took me down the hall to a room off the booking area. The first thing I noticed after I saw Peter, looking nervous and haggard, was that he had brought a friend.

A *friend*, for heaven's sake. Tom—the husband in the duo who had hosted Peter and my children over the weekend. I immediately began to turn away. To me this was just too much—utter degradation—on top of my horrific weekend.

Tom was an intensely intelligent, affable guy who happened to be a rocket scientist. Today he looked decidedly stern. The other man who was with them, who after a few moments I recognized from my church choir, firmly told me, "No." Meaning, I could not turn around and go back, which right then seemed preferable to sitting down with these people, shackled and in my orange jumpsuit and slippery socks. I would have preferred to have hung out a little longer with Vanessa.

Apparently this choir member was a judge, and probably not so hard to track down on a Sunday, where I imagined he was easily found in the choir loft.

I had no choice but to sit down with them all. Tom's presence was one of the most shameful details of my jail stay. I think they said he was there for "accountability" or some mumbo jumbo. Either way, he seemed content in his role and sat quietly looking on, I suppose taking astute mental notes, while everyone else took turns lecturing me. Even in my guilty, agitated state of mind, I knew Tom did not belong in a deeply personal, maritally rooted situation.

The judge seemed proud to be doing me the enormous personal favor of springing me out of here on Sunday instead of making me wait until the beginning of the week. (And doing me a favor he was.) He blamed the whole episode of Friday night on me, just like the police. Naturally, Peter had had lots of time to educate the larger community.

"I know it is fun to feel young in your job at the fitness center," the judge told me. I had no idea what he was talking about. To be sure, I was in great physical shape from strength training and swimming during breaks in those few morning hours I worked. But teaching preschoolers to swim, and making sure irresponsible teen-agers show up for their lifeguard shifts, much less pay attention to the pool, makes you feel incredibly old.

I heard all about my transgressions. I am not saying I do not have glaring character flaws, but some of these were quite new to me. Then Peter lectured me on some other issues that came to mind. These would later form the divorce strategy that ultimately did not work for him.

Tom sat calmly, as if he had nothing better to do on Sunday morning than watch this spectacle of humiliation. This was beginning to resemble the witch hunt many of these set-ups are.

The judge said he would lift the restraining order that accompanies a domestic violence-related arrest on one condition: that I agree to go to one of two rehab centers. This had to happen before my court date. What I was being rehabbed for was, and still is, unclear. It was also up to Peter if he would waive the three-day restraining order, so I could go home that day. He agreed.

Obviously, I was going to sign whatever was required for my release. I signed, donned my jeans and tie-dyed shirt once again, and relished the sound of the prison doors clanging shut behind me. I walked outside into the Sunday afternoon sunshine, silently determined to get out of my marriage—with my children in tow—as quickly as possible.

Kate's Story

"My soon to be ex-husband had me arrested last May. We were living in Massachusetts and were separated at the time, yet going through marriage counseling 'trying' to make it work. We had been together for seven years, married for four.

"One evening, David was spending time with the children at the marital home while I stayed overnight with a friend. I admit I was snooping and hacking a little on my laptop and managed to get my hands on some emails between him and a girl who worked for him, who I had been suspicious of. The emails clearly defined the sexual relationship and confirmed my hunch. We had been in marriage counseling the entire length of this affair which appeared to have been going on for about six months, and he'd just been blaming everything that came up on me. After putting up with months of verbal abuse from him and constant denials he did anything wrong, I was shocked to find absolute proof.

"I drove back to the house and confronted David in the garage. 'Please just be honest with me so we can both move forward,' I pleaded. He said some truly nasty things to me, all the while still denying the affair. 'You're crazy,' he said, looking me in the eye. 'That's why I can't stand to be with you anymore.'

"I lost it and slapped him across the face. He threw me to the ground. I tried to get up, but he pinned me down. He yelled toward the house for our children—an infant, a toddler and a pre-teen—to get the phone and call 9-1-1. The children just sat there, shocked and crying hysterically, as they watched me on the floor of the garage trying to get up, with David standing over me.

"David never directly hit me during the marriage, but he was a violent person. We lived in four houses during our relationship, and in every one, he punched holes in the walls and did other destructive things in front of the children and me. He was physically abusive to our dog.

"He finally allowed me to get up. I went to comfort my children, especially my toddler, who was raving. I picked him up. David told me to leave the house immediately, or he was calling the cops. I walked over to him to hand him our son, but my husband refused to take him. He forced me to put my screaming baby on the floor of the garage and back away. I felt like a monster. It was so painful to do that, and looking back it doesn't make sense as to why I complied. But as you can see, he was perfectly willing to call the cops. It still makes me feel ashamed but all I can say is he is a manipulative and controlling person. I never realized how much power he had over me until now.

"I got in my car to return to my friend's. My 9-year-old daughter ran out of the house, crying, 'Mom, I want to go with you!' We went away to my friend's house. About 45 minutes later, the cops showed up. They asked me about the incident, and I admitted to my participation in slapping him. Then they arrested me, saying they had no choice. (Massachusetts has adopted a 'preferred arrest' stance.)

"I will never forget the feeling of the handcuffs being clinked around my wrists. Who knew real handcuffs were so heavy? I have never been so humiliated in my entire life. I had never been arrested for anything prior to this.

"Fortunately, I was released immediately. It was just processing paper work, finger printing, and so on, and then waiting for someone to post bail and pick me up. I think I was at the station for two or three hours.

"Though the time I spent in there was brief, I was terribly ashamed. The whole experience made me an emotional wreck. But I guess it was no worse than the other things he did leading up to the arrest.

"David refused to drop the charges, and I am currently on unsupervised probation for six months for assault and battery, until my trial date. He owns his own business and easily works 80 hours a week. Since my youngest children were born, I have been a stay-home mom. I estimate he spent an average of 10 hours a week with the children during the marriage, including weekends. But when we went to court for temporary custody, he told the judge I was violent, an alcoholic, you name it.... With the police documentation to back him up, he currently has my children more hours a week than I do. Yet, he is still working, so my mother-in-law has my children most of this time. It kills me, and there is nothing I can do about it until our divorce hearing.

"As long as I do not violate probation, the charges should be dismissed. After that, my lawyer is going to work on expungement. After the arrest, I did have to call 9-1-1 once, after he slammed my arm into his car door. I called because I felt I had to do something or he would find a reason to call and have me arrested again. The police determined it was an accident.

"I am in counseling, and as part of my probation, I must continue with the therapy. The emotional impact has been the hardest for me to bear. This experience made me question everything, and worst, it made me question everything about myself. The whole ordeal is indescribable, and I pray that it will make me a wiser, stronger woman in the end. I feel I do not have anything to hide, and that he is the one that should be embarrassed. I know I am a respectable woman, and a dedicated mom."

4

"A CONTINUING AND BEWILDERING PARADOX"

"Laws are like cobwebs, which may catch small flies but which let wasps and hornets break through." —Jonathan Swift

A 2006 article in the scholarly journal *Violence Against Women* studied this "continuing and bewildering" paradox in the criminal justice system: "As policy is implemented to benefit a class of citizens who are traditionally underserved, once placed, the system seems to generate negative consequences, especially for that class of citizens the policy is designed to benefit."[12]

A study of gender disparities in California arrest rates for domestic violence between 1987 and 2000 found female arrest rates increased more than 500 percent—that is, in 1987, women comprised 5

---

[12] William DeLeon-Granadas, William Wells and Ruddyard Binsbacher. "Arresting Developments: Trends in Female Arrests for Domestic Violence and Proposed Explanations." *Violence Against Women*, Sage Publications. Vol. 12 Number 4 April 2006 355-371 Sage Publications. Print.

percent of all domestic violence arrests, and by 2000, 18 percent—according to the research.

The team outlined possible explanations for these unintended consequences, which included the possibilities of more violence by females and/or less violence by males; male manipulation of the system; more egalitarian response on the part of law enforcement; and an organizational backlash effect.

Male manipulation and backlash effect emerged as the most likely driving forces in this study. Most law enforcement officers I interviewed echoed this opinion, except for a couple who truly felt some women had increasingly violent tendencies, and they were finally being identified. "There is some evidence to suggest that male domestic violence suspects have become rather adept at making the most of any existing bias in the system, especially by influencing decisions made by officers at the scene of the crime," the report noted. "Observations of police interactions with domestic violence victims and suspects in Tempe, Arizona, revealed an often-subtle but powerful language emerged that conspired against female victims and helped male suspects to minimize their actions, deny responsibility, and shift blame."[13]

Jeffrey Smallwood, the former Orange County officer, said most Florida Certified Police Officers receive over 800 hours of training in all aspects of Florida law and procedure, including domestic violence, which he identified as "the second deadliest encounter a law enforcement officer can meet." (The first is traffic stops, he said.) Florida law requires constant in-service training and re-certification every four years, in which DV training is part of the core. The police learn how to resolve a

---

[13] Ibid.

problem quickly at a potentially dangerous, chaotic scene, pressure of time constraints and supervisors. Florida is a mandatu arrest state.

"To teach discernment is impossible with humanity," Smallwood acknowledged. "Academic credentials prove nothing, and common sense is subjective. Let me say this, after 20 years I had a sense, and more wisdom than I did when I started. Age is no substitute for wisdom, but I still made mistakes. Every officer should look at the totality of the scene. The verbiage, the conversation, the house, the injuries or marks if there has been violence. All this adds up to who is arrested. Have we arrested the wrong person? I bet we have."

Several factors might contribute to a mistaken arrest, Smallwood said, including a supervisor who rushes his officers to leave the scene when several cars have responded; a backup of 9-1-1 calls; or a verbally abusive person who is unable to articulate his or her side of the matter and becomes abusive to the responding officers. All may play a part.

Smallwood agreed the situation of a man setting up his wife can also be at play. "Sometimes there is the male 'machismo' thing that gets in the way of discerning the truth of the matter and sometimes the 'God with a badge' syndrome affects our tender egos. We might jump too soon on an arrest, but you must remember we do not have the luxury of spending an entire shift on the scene attempting to decide who is at fault or who the aggressor is. We are responders who do not have the time detectives do to decide the arrest."

This is one of the problems of a "mandatory arrest" policy, he added. "Legislators who pass such laws seldom ask those on the front ϡ police officers, what they think before they bow to

ϡbby and pass a law."

.'urthering the Abuse

Marie DeSantis' website, *www.justicewomen.com*, stresses that despite the devastation a woman experiences after such an incident—which often is an extension of existing emotional or other abuse—she needs to gather support where she can in order to stay on her feet and fight back.

"Victims of domestic violence who get arrested are usually shattered emotionally, much more so than domestic violence victims who have not been arrested," DeSantis reports. "On top of the trauma of the domestic violence itself, the injustice of the arrest is unbearable to most women. And worse, if the woman has children, she is usually fearful that the perpetrator will use this arrest to go into family court and get custody of the children... All told, a domestic violence victim who has been arrested is often in such a broken mental state that she's unable to focus on the steps she must take to save herself."[14]

In her work helping women clear their records, Tamara Holder does not dabble in emotional territory, and instead encourages women to maintain a network of friends, to keep their relationships going. She will need them later. "I don't offer emotional resources," Holder said. "I tell women this: 'I am your attorney and your counselor at law. You have emotional issues that you must recognize, and you must seek counsel on how to deal with the abuse. But, we must remove the emotion from my

---

[14] DeSantis, *www.justicewomen.com*

job. You are investing in me because I'm going to help you clear up a legal blemish that could potentially scar you for life.'"

She continued, "I'm very straight up. No time for tears. I have a job to do: clean up this criminal mess so that you can move forward. Prove to that bastard that what he did to you will not haunt you forever. Forever! Think about it: The effect of a domestic battery conviction is like cutting off someone's finger. It's permanent!"

The best thing one can do is invest in all forms of assistance available and rise above the perpetrator, she said. "It's a complicated web, not for one person to fix."

In instances like mine, when the arrest and what follows might be considered more the result of "divorce gamesmanship" than what most would consider serious domestic abuse, I can vouch that the fear of losing custody on top of the shame of such an arrest is still all-consuming. It abruptly skews the former, if tentative, equilibrium you might imagine you have when the possibility of divorce begins to take root. Disturbing events begin to happen with jarring frequency, and you might start to wonder if you ever knew your new "opponent" at all. You are afraid to move, lest you find your foot in another trap.

This is typical.

For women in abusive relationships encountering these tactics, only the testimony of women in this book helps me begin to imagine the state of mind an unjust arrest on undeserved charges on top of the existing emotional turmoil would create.

The Violence Against Women Act

Congress passed the Violence Against Women Act of 1994 (VAWA 1994) as part of the Violent Crime Control and Law Enforcement Act of 1994. VAWA is a comprehensive legislative package designed to end violence against women. It was reauthorized in 2000 and 2005 and passed through the Senate in March 2012, but there was still dissension over how grant monies are spent and proposed amendments including expanding protection for same-sex couples, rural and Native American communities, and immigrants. VAWA 2000 authorized $3.2 billion in spending over five years. VAWA 2005 reauthorized the grant programs, adding more to include areas such as dating violence; violence against Indian women and youth; and strengthening federal criminal laws.[15]

VAWA was designed to improve criminal justice responses to domestic violence, sexual assault, and stalking, and to increase the availability of services for victims of these crimes. The community players who are supposed to work together to increase the system's effectiveness include police officers, prosecutors, judges, probation and corrections officials, health care professionals, leaders within faith communities, and survivors of violence against women. When instated, the federal law combined tough penalties to prosecute offenders—bringing domestic violence from the social realm to the criminal—while implementing programs to help the victims of such violence.

---

[15] "2006 Biennial Report to Congress on the Effectiveness of Grant Programs Under the Violence Against Women Act." *U.S. Department of Justice Office on Violence Against Women* (2006): 6. Print.

The Office on Violence Against Women (OVW) is a part of the United States Department of Justice and was created specifically to implement VAWA and subsequent legislation. This department allocates grant funds for implementing mandatory or pro-arrest programs and policies; developing policies and training in criminal justice agencies to improve tracking of domestic violence and dating violence cases; and creating centralized domestic violence units within police, prosecution, or other criminal justice agencies.[16]

The Violence Against Women Department requires detailed progress reports before it considers grant requests. They do not monitor police incident reports.[17] Instead, OVW officials report they draw on data collected by the Department of Justice and the FBI.

Since 1994, OVW has awarded more than $4 billion in grant funds to state, tribal, and local governments, nonprofit victim services providers, and universities.

Source: U.S. Dept. of Justice Office on Violence Against Women
You can find the most current information about the OVW's grant programs at *http://www.ovw.usdoj.gov/ovwgrantprograms.htm.*

---

[16] Ibid., 9.

[17] According to Traci Rollins-Johnson of the Department of Justice Violence Against Women office, OVW grantees must submit detailed semi-annual or annual progress reports regarding grant-funded activities. "Those jurisdictions that receive funding to engage in law enforcement activities do report arrest numbers, but they do not submit actual police reports," she said. For more detailed information on OVW's progress report system: the VAWA Measuring Effectiveness Initiative's website, *http://muskie.usm.maine.edu/vawamei/index.htm.*

5

A VICIOUS CATCH-22

"The strictest law sometimes becomes the severest injustice."
—Benjamin Franklin

Ashley's Story

"We lived in a Midwestern officer discretion state when this happened to me, but as you will see, I was arrested even though they could not find probable cause. I was 41. My husband had a high-profile, well paying job in the print news industry, and my 6-year-old son was successfully finishing treatment for leukemia. I had been a stay-home mom for six years before becoming business manager for our church. Our marriage had been seriously strained for a long time, and I had even filed for divorce earlier, but dropped it. I realized I still needed my husband, John, for benefits and income, because the area we live in is extremely expensive, yet we had to stay close to our son Evan's doctors.

"John married later in life than his friends—we have a 10-year age difference—and while his friends are now more free as their children grow older, I think having the young children held John back from lots of his past activities. He had also suffered a neck injury. I think he began to feel powerless to be no longer able to contribute and do what he wanted to do, and he started not to handle anything well. In counseling, the psychologist diagnosed him as bipolar with narcissistic personality disorder. Obviously, it created an unhealthy mix.

"So though I had filed for divorce from him before, I chickened out of the whole thing. I decided to change my expectations. John had previously been charged with domestic violence and received two orders of protection, which are court orders that restrict an abuser and are only available to families or household members. Both of these involved incidents with our older son Paul, who was in second grade at the time. A part of the reason I could justify staying, however, was because John did seem sick. And, on some level, Evan's serious illness created a diversion too.

"The night of my arrest, I was coming off a demanding and stressful holiday season with my job, and I needed to go to a business meeting. Unable to get a sitter, I persuaded John to take a day off. Now, though typically he did not do well with Paul, I was delighted to return home from my meeting that night and find Paul's homework completed, and dinner and dishes done too! But just as I was marveling at all this, John made it clear: 'I'm off duty.' He opened a bottle of wine, had a fire going, the whole 'Didn't I do good?' bit.

"I guess it could have been a relaxing and even romantic evening, but the children kept getting up. While I was upstairs trying to settle Evan down, I heard John yelling in the kitchen, just flying off the handle. Paul was down there with him. He was getting big for his age, and they were squaring off.

"Knowing all the violent things that had happened between them, I just reacted. I got between them. John had that look in his eyes—

he was not present—it was like blind rage. I saw that look, that clenched jaw, and I slapped him across the face. He just looked at me like, 'I can't believe you just did that.'

"It did work to stop the fight between him and Paul. I remember fleetingly thinking to myself, 'This does feel good.' Boy, did that feeling pass quick! I sent Paul upstairs again, reassuring him, 'We can talk about this later.'

"The next thing I knew, John was in the front doorway, and he was just incensed. He had the phone in his hand. 'I wonder how you think this would feel,' he said. The kids were up again, at the top of the stairs, hysterical. We knew what the threat was: that he would call 9-1-1.

"Paul was yelling, 'Mom was sticking up for me! You don't call the police on someone who was protecting you!'

"'I didn't really call,' John said with a laugh. 'I was just scaring you.' I begged, 'Please, let me get them to bed. Let me get these kids to sleep.'

"After a little while, John returned with the taunting. 'If you leave, if you do anything, no one gets to stay in the house. No one,' he said. This is a manifestation of his egotism and controlling nature. I looked at him and asked, 'Why can't you stop? If you can't stop doing this, I will put the boys in the car and go somewhere. Or I need you to leave and calm down.'

"So he left. Down the street he went. I reassured the boys and finally got them to sleep. When he had left, he had to move my car to get out, so I went outside to move it back into the driveway. Then up pulled two police cars.

"Well, John had driven to the police station. 'Your husband told us he had a detached retina from a fight,' the police said. The two police officers entered the house. They talked to me separately.

"'Where is the alcohol we heard about?' they asked. The bottle of wine John had opened was empty, and my still-full glass still sat on the mantelpiece. I could tell they were not buying that I was responsible for whatever had happened here.

"When they asked if I slapped John, I admitted it. I was confident they believed me and would let the matter go or suggest something other than arrest. But to my dismay, they informed me they had to arrest me. They even both called their boss, pleading for an exception to what was apparently an unwritten rule because we were in an officer-discretion state. 'There has to be some exception,' I heard them say. But at least in my case, there was none.

"'Who can come over and be with your children?' they asked me. So I called a friend who is also a coworker. The police put my kids in the cruiser and drove them to her house. John was cleared to come home, and I got booked and spent the night in a jail cell. The next day I was transported in handcuffs to the courthouse.

"I was a no-show at work for the first time in three years. Tongues were beginning to wag. But my friend got there and covered for me.

"The public defender did not say much except I was to appear in another court in two weeks, when they could throw out the charge. The judge deemed it a false arrest. But there was still an order of protection against me. The public defender looked embarrassed when she relayed a message from my husband. 'He says he'll drop the charges if you come back, talk to him, and apologize,' she said with a weak 'I don't get it either' smile. 'He says you also need to promise you won't get your record expunged because he needs it against you in case you file for divorce.' It was obvious to both of us that this was utterly absurd.

"I was like, 'Just get me out of here.' My only thought was my kids. I was so disappointed with myself. I felt I should have restrained myself. This is the problem. You blame yourself. So I told the state attorney, 'Fine, I will say whatever. Just get me out of this.' I went before the judge and he let me go. I was still in shock.

"When I arrived home, John greeted me at the front door. He obviously wanted to hear the apology. I just looked at him. He did not, and will not, get an apology from me for a situation he created.

"Now I am just concerned about preserving my reputation, and worrying that if I cannot get my record expunged, credit checks and background checks will destroy my future. I stayed in the marriage for economic reasons, but now my personal economic potential is far worse.

"The other thing I struggle with is the social stigma. I work for a church. My arrest made it into the blotter column of the local newspaper. My employers, fortunately, were sympathetic. Their opinion was that this is a private matter. But one of the teacher's aides reported seeing the blotter online. I am sure there is no environment worse for this kind of thing than a church, with that 'holier than thou' thing.

"This whole experience has made me feel the need to defend my character, for the first time in my life. I have tried to keep everything private. I did not make a big to-do. I did not want people to be afraid of their children coming to my home for a play date. These strikes against

me impact my children. And what do you do about work, for the sake of
your children?"

In 2008 VAWA's Arrest Program began tracking conviction rates for
domestic violence charges by the number of cases filed.[18]
Conviction rates for both misdemeanor and felony domestic
violence charges generally hover at a little over 50 percent, which would
help explain why many of us were able to have our charges dismissed and
records expunged, given the proper legal tools. (With all the paperwork
and legal counsel required, expungement is big business these days. See
Appendix B for a list of expungement—or the equivalent—guidelines for
each state.)

Those who can have their charges dismissed and expunged are
quite fortunate, but this does not mean there are no legal, social,
emotional, and financial hurdles to face in between the charges and the
dismissal. Further, some states, like Arizona, are "no drop states," in
which the case must go to trial regardless.

Remember my sentence to a treatment facility? This was just the
first step I had to take, entirely on my own, in having my charges
dropped and cleared. (What we signed in the jail was an agreement on
Peter's part that I could go back to my home without the standard three-
day plus waiting period.) The road out of this whole mess was long and
hard. After I successfully completed my nebulous "treatment"—which I
actually enjoyed in large part because it got me out of the house—I had to
hire a divorce attorney, and a crackerjack one. He in turn found a

---

[18] "2010 Biennial Report to Congress on the Effectiveness of Grant Programs
Under the Violence Against Women Act." 105.

criminal defense attorney for me, and I had to go to court. Those charges were dropped, but I still faced a contentious divorce and custody battle in which Peter seemed to want it all: boys, house, life as we knew it up until then, and everything else.

In between, I had to be uncharacteristically perfect, not even so much as indulging in a single glass of wine at a friend's house; take care of the boys; work my fitness center job as if nothing was wrong; and figure out how to find a full-time job so I could afford to keep things afloat. Peter's attorney apparently had encouraged him to tie up his paycheck in a new account I could not touch, and the considerable equity in our house had been drained for his legal counsel. My mother had to reach into her savings to give me the $40,000 my lawyers cost. After all these things were settled, I was a barely functioning wreck, but I set about getting my record expunged so I would be employable. I am grateful to live in a state where it is not too difficult. But it takes time, usually at least a year.

And then, on top of this was the burden of keeping up appearances—read, keep it all a secret—to virtually everyone but my mother and two friends, and now, mercifully, Jessica, who'd stepped back in my life just in time.

Jessica's post-jail experience was different, despite the attorney her parents ushered her to immediately on her release. In her words: "I was too emotionally crushed to pursue leaving. At that point, my self esteem was so low I honestly couldn't see what I had to offer anyone."

"Zero Tolerance" and the Children

Cristina Rathbone's book A *World Apart: Women, Prison, and Life Behind Bars* explores the reasons behind the staggering increase in the ranks of women doing time in America's prisons. A major cause of this is stringent "zero tolerance" laws requiring minimum drug offender sentencing (another scenario in which the punishment often does not fit the crime). Another, it seems evident now, must be the sometimes misguided arrests on simple assault charges. Of the women incarcerated today, 72.8 percent are serving time for nonviolent offenses, Rathbone wrote, while "of the 28 percent who are deemed violent, three-quarters are incarcerated for 'simple assault'—the lowest rung on the ladder of violent crimes."[19]

Moreover, she continued, "An astonishing 68 percent of incarcerated women are found to be clinically depressed when they are examined in prison—a statistic probably exacerbated by the fact that approximately two thirds are mothers and were the primary caretakers of children before being sent away."

The result? More than 1.3 million children in America are living without their mothers because they are incarcerated, Rathbone estimates. I found in writing this book that this statistic becomes even sadder when you factor in how many mothers lose custody of their children after just a short stint in jail. They do not have legal power, they are suddenly cut off from the marital assets, and their criminal charges can severely hobble their hopes of making their own living.

---

[19] Rathbone, Cristina. *A World Apart: Women, Prison, and Life Behind Bars.* New York: Random House: 2005, p. 22. Print.

Holder said she sees this every day in her Chicago office. "Battered women continuously call me to help get their records expunged, but they can't pay for my services. And, without their records expunged, they cannot secure jobs and earn money," she said. "It's a vicious Catch-22."

6
A FUNNY THING HAPPENED ON THE WAY TO EXPUNGEMENT

"Half the harm that is done in the world is due to people who want to feel important. They don't mean to do harm, but the harm does not interest them... or they do not see it, or they justify it... because they are absorbed in the endless struggle to think well of themselves."
—T.S. Eliot

Within a week after I returned home, Peter arranged for me to go to a rehab center, as per the conditions of my jail release. My goal was to strike off that requirement before my court date; his apparent purpose emerged soon enough. By this point, Peter's actions seemed even more coached and determined by pure strategy.

The judge had given me two choices of acceptable facilities. Only one was on the insurance, Appleford (a fictitious name), so it was an easy decision. Besides, it had a good name; their website did not look too bleak; and they seemed to cover all the bases.

Among their treatment offerings: Electroconvulsive Therapy (ECT); Addiction Intermittent Explosive Disorder; Borderline Personality Disorder/Schizophrenia; Dissociative Disorders/Delusional Disorders; and Post Traumatic Stress Disorder. Perhaps Appleford had something to offer me after all.

Under Peter's ever-watchful supervision, I packed my largest suitcase, carefully and tearfully choosing the children's notes and pictures I wanted to take with me. I put in some books.

There were strict guidelines for other belongings I was allowed to pack:

o   *3 Casual Outfits*
o   *Tennis Shoes/No Shoestrings*
o   *3 pairs Socks*
o   *3 pairs Underwear*
o   *2 T-shirts, 2 Long Sleeved Shirts*
o   *Robes with all inside strings not attached/ No belt allowed*
o   *Bras, Underwear*
o   *Appropriate Nightwear (not see thru or revealing)*
o   *Jacket/No Strings attached to it*
o   *Shampoo, Conditioner*
o   *Toothbrush, Toothpaste*
o   *Comb, Brush*
o   *Hair Dryer and Curling Iron*
o   *Swimming Attire*

These I dutifully put in, including the "swimming attire." I had no idea what I would be doing in a swimsuit, but it sounded like a pleasant diversion. I packed my goggles just in case.

When we arrived at the clinic at the appointed time, the admitting administrator was clearly puzzled about the overstuffed suitcase I was lugging. "She's staying for at least two weeks, right?" Peter asked anxiously.

I will never forget the look on the administrator's face. She stared at Peter. "This is an outpatient program," she said. Turning to me, she said, "You'll be going home today and coming in mornings until early afternoon, starting Tuesday."

Peter looked crushed that he was not going to be able to leave me there after all. I completed some paperwork in the administrator's office. When she took my blood pressure, it was through the roof.

I reported to Appleford the following Tuesday at 8:30 a.m. It was a daily program—including weekends. That first day I was exceedingly nervous, still a little banged up and shell shocked, but I began to relax when I saw how resigned and quiet the other people were and how laid back the place was. There was nothing sinister about it. This was not jail.

I actually came to enjoy going to Appleford. During my commutes, I alternated between the Evita soundtrack, Nickel Creek, and Nanci Griffith (ever my ally in tough times). I was most of all relieved my classes let out in time for me to spend every afternoon with the boys. They were at summer day camp for most of my schedule anyway.

I talked to people, compared lower back tattoos, went to classes, and took notes. I had an itinerary each day; it was a relief just to go from class to class, not to have to make any decisions. I chatted a lot (I always chat a lot). The food was excellent. People were at Appleford for vastly differing issues—I quickly learned the careful delineation between who was in the inpatient program and who was in an outpatient program. One tremendously sad inpatient woman had attempted suicide several times. Another was a troubled young man who killed the family cat, among other things, and could not forgive himself. Most sought help for drug and alcohol problems. I learned some about anger and stress management. I looked forward to Tai Chi on Sundays, and the wonderfully Zen, Rastafarian instructor.

I did not make any lasting friends, but most people were cordial, especially a kind man who remarked how lucky my husband was to have such a marvelous, beautiful wife. He asked me about the bruises on my arms and shins. "Fell down the stairs," I explained. He just shook his head.

❧

On Mother's Day, the clinic permitted me to take the day off. The highlight of that glorious day was playing with the boys in the backyard, swinging in the sunshine, so happy to be home with them for the entire day. The scene would have been idyllic had Peter not been standing there the whole time, smiling indulgently, arms folded, as if I were trying out for a babysitting job. He seemed robotic; I continued not to recognize him.

It eventually became clear that Appleford was a facility that keeps you until your insurance taps out. I begged to be discharged because I wanted to return to work and I worried I would be fired. In the evenings, I tried to occupy my boys—and myself—with simple projects from JoAnn and Michael's. We mostly did paint by number, a rote, mindless activity that was about the most inspiration I could manage. I did not have the focus to read or cross stitch, and we could paint together. I number-painted a cozy cottage at twilight, lights softly glowing in the windows, bordered with lovely lavender bushes and shrubbery in a sensory-overloading array of shades of violet and green in dozens of little plastic paint pots. The finished product did not look much like a Thomas Kinkade work, as the paint-by-number designer probably intended, but it was comforting. I willed my sons and me to that peaceful place.

I still had no formal diagnosis, but the therapists and the psychiatrist I saw were supportive. (The Appleford staff also later came in handy with notes and testimony for my hearing, in which I needed to convince a judge I was not a violent person. One staffer rescued me from a perilous situation not long after my discharge.)

After a while, when I had run out of things I could think of to talk about in group therapy, Sam, the lead counselor, put me in charge of the conversation whenever something cropped up that required him to leave the room. I will never forget an exchange I tried to moderate between a woman being treated for codependency, and a compulsive shopper. "I need a ride to Wal-Mart after this," the shopper declared. "I'll take you!" the codependent eagerly piped up.

Only a couple of days after I was discharged from Appleford, which was just shy of three weeks, Peter and I had a row while I was driving in traffic. It was a typical heated argument about why he was seeking sole custody of the children.

"Over my dead body," must have been one of my retorts. (Unfortunately, I had not yet internalized what I learned in Anger Management.)

On arriving home, I went to the backyard, which had become my office, to make a cell phone call.

Through the slats in the backyard fence I saw a new female pastor at our church—it took me a few moments to place her—pull up in her car in front of the house. She was already a client of Peter's side business, in which he sold expensive, high-quality stationery. The ministry obviously has a penchant for fancy writing paper. I thought she was coming to purchase a journal or something.

Then the cops came. Peter must have directed them to me because they stormed into the back yard, guns pulled. "Um, I'll have to call you back," I gushed into my cell phone. "The cops are here again."

The police, a male and a female officer, questioned me about a cement block next to a tree in the yard, and implied that I might aspire to step up and hang myself from it. "I don't know what you're doing here. I've not done anything, and I'm not going to do anything," I protested. I still do not know what that block was doing there.

I ran to Peter, who was watching from the back gate, and implored him, "Help me! Tell them to leave and that I didn't do anything! *Help me!*" Peter had that crazy vacant stare. He said nothing, refusing to meet my eyes. The police took me inside, separating us. By now, I knew this drill. The female officer sat with me in the living room. I understood I was not permitted to walk away.

From the armchair where I sat, I could see out the large living room windows into the front yard. The minister was watching my children outside. Suddenly I understood her role. Peter had arranged for a babysitter while I was being terrorized. He had obviously called the church office and reported I was threatening suicide. They got to call 9-1-1 this time.

"You've got issues," the female cop was telling me. "You need to get some balls." I do believe she meant this constructively, and I still try to remember that advice. Then I had an idea: If I could get to a phone, I could get them to consult someone who knew me from Appleford. I told the police such a person could confirm I was not suicidal, nor violent.

It was a late Friday afternoon, and to this day, I feel pure joy and relief at tracking down Sam, the group therapy counselor, on the phone. He asked to speak with the lead officer. Sam must have told them something along the lines of, "If you want crazy, you've got the wrong person," and that it was a set-up. Obviously, Peter was trying to get me locked up again, so he could continue building his divorce case without my interference.

The party finally dispersed. Everybody left. I was so angry with that minister who foolishly let herself get played, and I was equally mad at whoever Peter had manipulated into dialing 9-1-1 from the church. (Now I am able to admit the minister in all likelihood had no idea what role she was truly playing.) But at the time, I felt betrayed, especially by my former church "friends" who furthered Peter's agenda by gossiping about me. I try to remember who set these events in motion, and consider it a firsthand example of how pernicious and powerful a distortion campaign truly is.

But I can say this: No one, not one, from that crowd asked for my side of the story, nor appeared to have given me the benefit of the doubt.

I suppose I could have stepped forward with my side of the story, but I did not have the energy to fight that tornado. I probably could not have changed its course.

∾

Even when you realize people—and this includes church members—are human after all, susceptible as anyone to gossip and hysteria, the effect can be profound on the subject. In my case, I no longer attend tightly programmed church services or activities, not because they have no value, but because I have discovered the calm, Light-filled meetings of the Religious Society of Friends (Quakers). I admire their peaceful outlook and focus on gutsy activism that creates a real example.

This stands out to me as the most destructive aspect of these divorce tactics: With the aid of the system, the core force—whatever or whoever it is that is creating it—gathers power, and, with it, followers who perpetuate it. Even coming from what should be the safest of places.

While many marriages end in divorce, one has to see up close what complications accompany those preceded by a 9-1-1 call: protective orders; restraining orders; loss of custody; social ostracization; job loss; emotional trauma; but, if you're lucky, maybe a stint in half-day rehab that ultimately turns out to rescue you.

Cut Off

A significant obstacle facing a stay-home mom or a mother who works part-time is she probably does not have her own money to fight in court.

If she is lucky, family can help. Often she has been cut off from the marital finances by the time her court date rolls around.

Alexis Moore, founder of Survivors in Action, a domestic violence (DV) reform organization in El Dorado Hills, California, agreed.

"There are many women who are incarcerated and end up 'losing' because they don't have the funding or resources that the male victims have when they are arrested and/or charged with domestic violence. The men have the purse strings, so once they are arrested, they can easily post bail, hire lawyers, and work the system. On the other hand, female victims don't have the same resources."

To make matters even worse, a long-term effect of a criminal charge is now beginning to emerge, as the cyber world shows that information—including criminal records—lingers forever. Even if a woman can get her record expunged—or the equivalent—the original incident report remains.

There is also the protective order. We should be alarmed that companies are coming up with policies that bar anyone who has had a criminal record at all. (See Sidebar.) The implication is clear: These terrific strikes against people who have been arrested can prohibit them from making a living for themselves and their children.

Many states host background check systems on their websites. Official criminal history records are readily available for subscribing employers to conduct online searches of employees. Prospective employees also are often required to sign a "right to know" waiver authorizing such searches.[20]

---

[20] "Alabama Criminal Justice Information Center - Citizens." N.p., n.d. Web. 8 June 2011. *http://www.acjic.alabama.gov/citizens.cfm*.

Tamara Holder takes issue with the "misconception" that dismissed cases are not visible to the public, and background check companies. "They are! And they matter," she said. "I always say this: 'Do you want your daughter dating a guy who was once arrested for domestic battery, regardless of the outcome?' Absolutely not. Employers feel the same way... Does an employer want to risk the liability that this person may go postal in the workplace? Hell no, especially when there are other candidates without an arrest. And no employer wants to hear the 'what happened was' story about some fight with the ex."

Many people do not realize how much more there is to an arrest than just that. "I find that many who are arrested encounter the sad fact that most lawyers and officials feel that an arrest doesn't matter to the person arrested, since it is not a conviction," said Moore. "Many think that a mere arrest can't hurt someone. However, since the inception of the Internet and with the mass amounts of information available today, having an arrest on one's record is just as damaging as being convicted. Many, including law enforcement, then use it against you. So truth being told, an arrest as well as convictions need to be expunged, which is not easy. It costs money to hire lawyers, and requires lots of time."

Sheer grace saved me because I was able to parlay my part-time job at the fitness center into a full-time job not long after my divorce was final. This provided not only a modest income and health insurance, but allowed me to keep my house on the boys' behalf. My background check had already been conducted when I joined the staff two years before. It would be a whole year before my record would be expunged. Jessica was planning to pursue a career in real estate at the time of her arrest and had to wait an entire year to enroll in real estate school because of her charges. (We had believed our expungements wiped out all evidence of the incidents, but our incident reports remain on record. We had no idea this was so until the writing of this book.)

Not all states offer the option of expungement, but many provide for an equivalent. Arizona, for example, does not allow formal expungement of criminal records. Records of crimes in that state remain on the offender's record until they reach age 99. The state recently added a statute allowing a person to petition to have his or her case "set aside." (See Appendix B for a complete breakdown by state.)

In Illinois, Holder explained, there are two options: an expungement and a sealing statute. But a significant problem is that most domestic battery cases have an order of protection attached to them, which can last for several years. "So the criminal case is dismissed but the civil order of protection—or 'OP', also called a restraining order—still stands."

"What employer wants to hire someone who has a restraining order against them?" she added. "It's a protective remedy telling the world: Johnny is so afraid of Jenny that the court must protect him for her." The OP is not part of a criminal case, but it is attached to the incident. The OP lingers long after the case is over.

Worst, since the OP is not a criminal matter, the expungement laws do not apply. "So say you get the domestic battery expunged because it was dismissed," Holder said. "The OP is still visible to the world... even if the OP was dismissed."

The system is fantastically complicated.

Bottom line, you do not have to have a conviction in order to show up in a background check. For instance, the state of Alaska's website states: "If you were arrested or charged with a crime and/or the charge was filed in court the charge will be shown on your criminal history report even if it was dismissed or declined for prosecution."[21]

Alaska will consider "sealing" the record, in which case the petitioner submits a written request, to the head of the agency responsible for maintaining information, asking the agency to seal such information that may have resulted from a false accusation.

The state of Delaware has adopted a progressive stance with overt empathy for innocent persons: "Arrest records can be a hindrance to an innocent citizen's ability to obtain employment, get an education or to obtain credit. This... is intended to protect innocent persons from unnecessary damage that may occur as the result of arrest and other criminal proceedings that are unconfirmed or unproven."[22]

The Case Must Go On

A common misconception is that if the "victim" does not want the case to proceed, then the arresting agency will drop it. "Not so," Holder said. "The case can always proceed without putting the complaining witness on the stand so long as they have other evidence. A perfect example is Chris Brown and Rihanna. Even if Rihanna didn't want prosecutors to proceed, they had other evidence besides her testimony to take it to trial."

---

[21]"Alaska Public Safety Statewide Services." N.p., n.d. Web. 26 June 2011. *http://www.dps.state.ak.us.*
[22] "Chapter 43. Sentencing, Probation, Parole and Pardons. Delaware Code Subchapter VII. Expungement of Criminal Records." N.p., n.d. Web. 7 March 2012. *http://delcode.delaware.gov/title11/c043/index.shtml*

In most of this chapter, we are talking about expungements for people whose charges were dropped. But if a person is convicted of domestic battery, most states do not allow for the expungement of that record, though there are some exceptions.

"Domestic battery is generally a misdemeanor, yet it can haunt someone forever," Holder added. "Employers definitely don't want to take the risk...whether the person's case was dismissed or the person was convicted. The arrest alone puts the fear of God in employers."

"I realize I need to get that expungement process going for multiple reasons," said Ashley, the Midwesterner whose husband firmly requested she not get her record expunged. "It apparently takes 120 days. I certainly don't want it thrown out because of a technicality, and have to start over again."

She could go back to her former divorce attorney to expunge her record, she admitted. "I know I just can't face an 'I told you so' lecture and the pressure to turn an expungement back into a divorce filing, when I don't have my financial ducks in a row to see the process through right now," she said. "I want the expungement taken care of first so it can't be fought by John's attorney, and used against me in a divorce."

Ashley still wishes the arresting officers had been given the flexibility to use their own judgment and not arrest her, when it was obvious they had doubts. "Like I said, they felt awful and spent the entire time from handcuffing me to locking the jail cell door apologizing over and over, explaining again and again that they had to follow the procedure since they were ordered to arrest me."

"Job Seekers With Criminal Records Need Not Apply"

The National Employment Law Project, a national advocacy group for the unemployed, released a report in March 2011 with troubling statistics: More than one in four American adults—about 65 million people—have an arrest or conviction that will show up in a routine criminal background check, "and many employers are routinely, and illegally, discriminating against them when they apply for jobs."

The NELP report, entitled "'65 Million Need Not Apply': The Case for Reforming Criminal Background Checks for Employment," surveyed online job ads posted on Craigslist.com in five major cities: San Francisco, Los Angeles, Chicago, New York, and Atlanta. The survey found examples of strict requirements that automatically eliminated anyone with a criminal record, in clear violation of federal civil rights law, according to NELP.

Major companies including Domino's Pizza, the Omni Hotel, and Adecco USA, listed entry-level jobs on Craigslist that unambiguously shut the door on applicants with criminal records. The positions ranged from warehouse workers to delivery drivers to sales clerks.

NELP cited ads that included verbiage like this:

o *"No Exceptions! ...No Misdemeanors and/or Felonies of any type ever in background"*

o *"DO NOT APPLY WITH ANY MISDEMEANORS / FELONIES"*

o   *"You must not have any felony or misdemeanor convictions on your record. Period."*[23]

NELP found more than 300 instances over four months in 2010 in which staffing agencies and employers, large and small, posted over-exclusionary job ads. Based on the findings, NELP concluded that there are easily thousands of postings by employers nationwide imposing blanket policies against hiring people with criminal records.

"These background checks are supposed to promote safety in the workplace, but many employers have gone way overboard, refusing even to consider highly qualified applicants just because of an old arrest or conviction," reported Christine Owens, executive director of NELP. "They're not even bothering to ask what the arrest or conviction was for, how far in the past it was, whether it's in any way related to the job, or what the person has done with his or her life since."[24]

Expungement Defined

In the common law legal system, an expungement proceeding is a type of lawsuit in which a first-time offender of a prior criminal conviction—or a person whose charges were dismissed—seeks that the records of that earlier process be sealed, thereby making the records unavailable through the state or Federal repositories. If successful, the records are

---

[23]Rodriguez, Michelle Natividad, and Maurice Emsellem. "'65 Million Need Not Apply': The Case for Reforming Criminal Background Checks for Employment." The National Law Employment Project, n.d. Web. 26 June 2011. *http://nelp.3cdn.net/e9231d3aee1d058c9e_55im6wopc.pdf*
[24] Ibid.

considered "expunged." Black's Law Dictionary defines "expungement of record" as the "Process by which record of criminal conviction is destroyed or sealed from the state or Federal repository." While expungement deals with an underlying criminal record, the process is a civil action in which the petitioner asks the court to expunge the records.

There is a difference between an expungement and a pardon. When an expungement is granted, the person whose record is expunged may, for most purposes, view the event as if it never occurred. A pardon (also called "executive clemency"), on the other hand, does not "erase" the event. Rather, it constitutes forgiveness. In the United States, only a judge can grant an expungement, while only a governor can grant a pardon for state offenses. Only the President of the U.S. can pardon federal offenses. In Nebraska, pardons are by a vote of the governor, attorney general, and secretary of state.

Each jurisdiction whose law allows expungement has its own definitions of expungement proceedings. Generally, expungement is the means to "remove from general review" the records pertaining to a case. In many jurisdictions, however, the records may not entirely "disappear" and may still be available to law enforcement; to sentencing judges on subsequent offenses; and to corrections facilities.

Requirements for expungement often include one or more of the following:

o   Fulfilling a waiting period between the incident and expungement;
o   Having no intervening incidents;
o   Having no more than a specified number of prior incidents;
o   That the conviction be of a nature not considered to be too serious;
o   That all terms of the sentence be completely fulfilled;

- o   That no proceedings be pending;

- o   That the incident was disposed without a conviction; and

- o   That the petitioner completes probation without any incidents.

Types of convictions that are often not eligible for expungement include:

- o   *Felonies and first-degree misdemeanors in which the victim is under 18 years of age;*

- o   *Rape;*

- o   *Sexual battery;*

- o   *Corruption of a minor;*

- o   *Sexual imposition; and*

- o   *Obscenity or pornography involving a minor.*

In some jurisdictions, all records on file within any court, detention or correctional facility, law enforcement or criminal justice agency concerning a person's detection, apprehension, arrest, detention, trial or disposition of an offense within the criminal justice system can be expunged. Each state sets its own guidelines for what records can be expunged, or for whether expungements are available at all. The petitioner requesting an expungement of all or part of their record will have to complete forms and instructions to submit to the appropriate authority. The petitioner may choose to hire an attorney to guide him or her through the process, or he or she can decide to represent himself or herself (this is referred to as "appearing *pro se*"). Contributing source: "Expungement—Findlaw's Criminal Law Center." N.p., n.d. Web. 26 June 2011. *http://criminal.findlaw.com/expungement/*

7

ON THE DISTORTION CAMPAIGN TRAIL

"Don't tell fish stories where the people know you; but particularly, don't tell them where they know the fish." —Mark Twain

S o I had been sprung from Appleford and avoided the second arrest scheme, but my court date loomed. During this time, my house had become an extremely scary place to be. I could feel the threats hovering, and I was anxious to get my court hearing behind me, so I could proceed with my divorce.

Around this time, a well-heeled friend of my mother's even offered to have a "root"—something like a hex—put on Peter. (The isolated Lowcountry islands are thick with voodoo, whose influence occasionally wafts in to town on a warm, salty breeze.) I rather regretted my declining her well-meaning offer on nights Peter would wander through the house with a flashlight, poking around. He would shine it through the crack under the door to the master bedroom downstairs, where I locked myself in every night. He was probably looking for random evidence of some kind, but it was frightening.

If I had had any notion of the ranks he was rallying to his side and the terrible stories circulating about me, I sometimes think I might have said "yes" to the root.

By this time, I had hired a divorce lawyer who not only was on his game but was a family-focused man—with a great reputation as one of Georgia's "Super Lawyers," and a strong track record. He was a highly respected player in the family law realm, often serving as a guardian ad litem (an attorney who represents children). He sometimes returned phone calls from the grocery store as he picked up dinner for his family. He posted homework help links on his corporate website. We agreed our strategy would be to stick to the straight and narrow—to look at everything through the lens of what was best for the children.

At this point, I was still so emotionally whipped that I truly believed I was going to be lucky to get joint custody, let alone primary. Peter was still gunning for the house and sole custody, leaving me... nowhere. He had gathered all our "couple friends" and all the church acquaintances to his side. The distortion campaign was in full swing.

When I was collecting character witnesses to bolster my case that I was a good person and a devoted mother, I confidently called up one of the primary ministers of our church (not the same associate pastor who "babysat" that day) to ask her if she would be willing to testify for me in writing. I had faithfully attended her popular Bible studies and retreats. She had seen me with my children often. I thought she felt she knew me personally, and thought well of me. I left her a detailed voice message.

She returned my call with what seemed to me a terse, indifferent voicemail: "I got your message and I feel bad for *all* of you. You will all be in my prayers." Then she hung up. It stung, and I was puzzled that, of all people, she would not vouch for me. She was one of Peter's customers too, however. I actually wondered if she had chosen decorative journals for her retreats over helping a desperate parishioner and her children. In more charitable moments, I concede it could have been a "boundary" issue for her. Either way, lack of support from someone you trusted simply hurts.

I decided I would focus on the only part of my life I could control: simply putting one foot in front of the other, and going through the motions of everyday life on my boys' behalf.

It was summer, and the fitness center provided a safe retreat. The boys went to the play center while I taught; then we played Marco Polo and dived for weighted sticks together. My sons were competent swimmers by this time, and could play on their own while I carried on divorce business on the pool deck, my new office. I could not wait to get the divorce settled and be free from the marriage and all its fetters, especially Peter. Even if I had to leave my home and live in a week-to-week motel with supervised visitation. That is how low my expectations had sunk.

But first, I had to get my criminal charges dropped.

My attorney had referred me to a criminal lawyer to represent me in the hearing for my domestic violence charges. I had no idea in the beginning, even after my arrest, I would need a second attorney to get me out of this. This guy turned out to have represented a couple of middle school girls who made national headlines after serving cornbread laced with glue and bleach to teachers and other students. I figured he could manage my case, but he was nearly impossible to reach by phone.

Meanwhile, I persuaded the Appleford professionals to attest to my nonviolent nature. I could tell the psychiatrist in particular was reticent about going on record, but I desperately needed his written documentation as well as my dismissal papers from Appleford, to show I had completed all my tasks like an obedient little girl. I was frantically worrying about whether I would even be able to reach this attorney in time to get everything into his hands. I had no idea what he even looked like by the time my court date rolled around.

I cannot remember if I asked anyone to attend my hearing with me, but I went to the local courthouse alone. I wore my newest sundress and kept my sunglasses on, I suppose, as a mask. I was early, and waited for at least two hours outside the courtroom. I paced the second-story balcony of the ornate courthouse lobby, frantically looking for a person who might be my attorney. I kept nervously checking with the guard positioned at the courtroom door to see if my literal number was up. As my turn inched closer, I became panicky. Finally, I had no choice but to take my seat on a well-worn bench toward the back of the room.

The ranks of humanity sharing space in that courtroom were diverse. All ages, ethnicities, apparent occupations, even children, were jammed into neat rows. I watched with a knot in my stomach as the judge called one case after another. There was no sign of anyone who looked like he might be looking for me.

Suddenly I spotted a familiar face atop an extremely tall body, across the room closer to the bench. Another choir member, a baritone. I had never seen many singers outside the choir rooms, and here they were marching through the most shameful part of my entire life. I shrunk in my uncomfortable seat, hoping he would not see me. I figured the baritone was probably there petitioning something trite like a traffic ticket. I was fearful my turn would come first, and he would hear my whole story.

Finally, after seemingly hours of rehearsing my "not guilty" pleas to myself, a man beckoned to me from the front of the courtroom. *"Where is my attorney?"* my psyche screamed. I could not believe that after all the bad breaks I had already experienced, even my phantasmic criminal lawyer had stranded me.

As I approached the bench on unsteady legs, my sunglasses perched on the end of my nose so I could see, I was surprised that I was not asked to approach the bench but waved around to a side door behind it. Bewildered, I followed.

Behind the door was my attorney. He introduced himself. He wore cowboy boots and a bolo tie. He had already conferred with the judge in His Honor's chambers, and had both my charges—simple battery and interference with a 9-1-1 call—dropped.

I never had to approach the bench or plead my case before the rest of the courtroom at all. I was so relieved, the tears streamed behind my amber-tinted lenses.

&

Peter's and my church friends were mostly a fun, party-oriented and children-focused bunch—there was nothing pious about them. Many attended our church because they wanted to sing in the choir, which was extremely accomplished, rowdy, and professionally led, and thus attracted people who liked to sing as much or more than pray. I was not as strong a singer as most of them, but I held my own in the alto section. I counted my fellow choir members as my closest social circle.

Immediately after my arrest, however, suddenly all contact with these friends evaporated. It did not help that Tom, the friend who took his Sunday morning off to come to the spectacle of my jail release, was one of them. He and his wife Meg, whom I had considered a close friend, had kept the boys while Peter figured out what was going on and consulted with his attorney. I realized I must be the subject of much gossip.

In the end, I identified what seemed my one real friend from this 1,500-member mega-church: Kristin, who finally confided that people were indeed talking about me, and saying terrible things. Humiliating pictures were circulating of our house at its messiest, inferring its chaotic state was due to my poor housekeeping skills, even as Peter worked from home. Most shaming to me were snapshots of some girls' night gag gifts I had received at one of those for-women-only "put the spark back in your sex life" parties (which was hosted by one of these former friends). I had not even taken those silly toys seriously enough to hide from anyone but the boys, but the pictures had the embarrassing effect intended.

In addition, Kristin had been present at a gathering Peter had attended without me, with my sons in tow. Vicious gossip about me reportedly flew as my children played within earshot.

The moment I heard about the gossip in front of my children, I immediately drove over to Peter's newly rented house. I asked the boys to go play outside and spoke with him in as low and controlled a voice as I could manage in my rage. I knew to keep it together, by then.

Obviously concerned I had gotten wind of all the quickly got on the phone with Tom.

A flurry of activity ensued wherein my ex-friends fretted over who leaked this information, which of course would make Peter look dirty in the divorce. Finally, two primary leaks were identified: Tom's wife Meg, and Barbara, a pretty, somewhat neurotic young woman with a lovely voice who had just earned her PhD. in psychology, of all things. I enjoyed a brief telephone interview with Barbara, whom I happily interrogated. I had attended every housewarming, every child's birthday, celebrated every milestone Barbara had had in the past several years. Now she was on the bash-me bandwagon? I quite contentedly left her in tears and passed the receiver back to Peter.

I had to swallow a chuckle as Peter asked Barbara, who must have been a mess, with conspiratorial concern: "Are you all right?"

After Peter hung up with the distraught Barbara, I told him, "If any of these people or anyone anywhere dares utter one more word about me when my children are present, I will have them all subpoenaed and use it as evidence that you, and your friends, are supporting a hostile environment."

The warning did at least shut this group up.

But the constant wondering plagued me for years. I wondered which of my neighbors—I remained in the house with the boys—Peter had gotten to and "educated" about me. After all, the cops had come not too terribly late on a Friday evening, when people were still coming and going, and walking their dogs. Practically every time I saw someone Peter and I both knew, I automatically thought, "Has she heard about me?" "Has that family heard about me?" The "not knowing" was driving me crazy. One neighbor who remained a friend and was well connected, and with whom I shared my early manuscript, reported she had heard nothing. Once a campaign like this is sprung about you, you assume everyone knows. I realize now that the fear, the threat "to tell," can be worse than the reality. The emotional damage is done.

Kill the Witch

My experience with a changeable community mob gives me the tiniest glimmer of how the 16th and 17th century witch hunters operated as they weeded out "wicked" people who threatened to taint their pious community.

Because I am a natural redhead—a common indicator one was a witch, in some medieval circles—I have always suspected I would not have had a prayer back in the day. Factoring in my natural reporter's inquisitiveness and a predilection for argument (particularly when wrongly accused), I think I would have been toast.

Interestingly, one of the explanations of "bewitchment" in the case of the children of Salem in 1692, whose testimony sent more than 20 men and women to their deaths (and which had, as far as I know, nothing to do with their hair color), has been attributed to psychological projection, the basis of a distortion campaign. Some modern historians argue the accusing girls had convulsive fits caused by repressed aggression and attention-seeking acting out, which they were able to project without blame because of the speculation swirling about witchcraft.[25] (Others have hypothesized the fits were caused by bad herbs; bread infected by a fungus from which LSD is derived; an epidemic of encephalitis, which resulted in the physical and neurological behaviors the "witnesses" displayed; and/or sleep paralysis. We will probably never know for sure.)

࿇

A vilification, or distortion, campaign is a carefully constructed string of manipulative actions designed to destroy the target's reputation as well as his or her relationships with family, friends, employers, coworkers, doctors, therapists, and anyone else related to the target. "The intent may even be to force the target to leave the community, put the target in prison, or even kill the target," according to one mental health website.[26] Such tactics are commonly associated with borderline or narcissistic personalities, but extreme men's rights websites encourage them as "divorce gamesmanship."

The wagerer of a distortion campaign will "use basically any means available to them to cause damage to his target, including denigration, endless disparaging remarks, fabrication, false accusations, and even teaching others (including their children!) to lie on their behalf as part of their vilification campaign."[27]

A woman whose husband or partner has her arrested can expect this sort of behavior to follow. A smear campaign can swiftly slice her life

---

[25] "Psychological projection." N.p., n.d. Web. 3 July 2011. *http://karlrwolfe.com/psychological-projection.html*
[26] "BPD Distortion Campaigns | angiEmedia." N.p., n.d. Web. 27 June 2011. *http://angiemedia.com/2008/12/29/bpd-distortion-campaigns*
[27] Ibid.

in two, separating all that has gone before—including friends, social alliances, even jobs—from what lies ahead. The lies and rumors are hurtful and further erode her flagging self esteem. This fuels the campaigner's goal, which is to crush her spirit. He gathers supporters to justify himself and even testify against his target in the divorce case. He hopes she will just crawl away and disappear so life may proceed the way he wishes.

In my interviews, I found it striking that each of the female victims of a 9-1-1 ploy had tried to protect her husband or significant other's reputation. (Stephanie's story at the end of this chapter is a perfect example of this.) I held back in my separate "interview" with the police the night I was arrested; I did not want *anyone* to get in trouble. I certainly did not want to see Peter hauled off to jail. (Obviously, I had no idea at the time he did not have that big a problem seeing *me* arrested.) I did not tell them that he had baited me. Other women reported additional fears of losing their husbands' livelihoods to arrests or tarnished reputations, even if they were deserved. This phenomenon— such a far cry from a distortion campaign—often occurs when women are stay-at-home moms.

This is another reason why, even if they choose to stay home with their children, women should strive to have their own money to put aside, and keep up their professional affiliations and certifications so they can quickly move back into a career if the need arises. They can also carve time in the nooks and crannies of their days to study for another line of work that interests them. (See How To Spot a Set-Up and What To Do for more ideas about accruing and saving "fall-back money.")

All women need to learn to recognize signs that they need to become more self-sufficient, and to protect themselves in proactive, not reactive, ways. They cannot wait until it is too late.

Stephanie's Story

"I had never called the police on my husband for two reasons: I felt the police had far more important things to do than break up a fight between a husband and wife, and I was stupidly protecting his reputation in the community and business world. I decided the smart and classy way to protect myself was to file for a DV Restraining Order. So I went to the Clerk of Court's office in my local community—I live in the Pacific Northwest—and filled out the papers. A DV Restraining Order forbids the person you're filing about to come near you or otherwise threaten you. I wanted to avoid the arrest route for lots of reasons, and thought just keeping him away would be sufficient to protect me.

"In a petition for a DV Restraining Order, you're supposed to tell your story very simply and clearly. You document the threats and explain why you fear this person will harm you. I put down the truth: My husband isolated me in a section of the home, putting padlocks on many of the rooms so I could not enter them. He shoved me and screamed obscenities at me. He took my belongings and removed valuable marital property from my home. He locked me out of joint files, and removed money from joint bank accounts. He even tampered with my food. He changed the password on my email account; disconnected my phone; and installed surveillance in our home to further terrorize me.

"The judge is supposed to read your petition, ask any questions, and carefully weigh the conditions of your request. He or she can grant your petition on the spot if it seems necessary. This was my hope. I had great faith in this carefully chosen course of action.

"Well, I tried to include everything but the judge threw out my request. She also ordered *me* out of the house, with no support! She stated, 'If all this were true, Mrs. Douglas, you would have called the police. So I do not believe you. I think you are fabricating lies against your husband. I deny your request. I award your husband the residence. You have to leave the home by the end of this month, and you must not remove any property from the home until your divorce hearing.'

"She even added that I would have to split the marital pets with my husband. And that he got first pick of the dogs.

"I advise anyone in a similar situation to fully investigate the definition of what constitutes domestic violence by your local laws. In my case, the shoving and verbal abuse would have been enough. You should call the cops if your spouse has committed domestic abuse or violence towards you, including and especially if you are going through a divorce. *Do not hesitate to call the cops, as I did.*"

Elements of a Classic Distortion Campaign

The perpetrator of a distortion campaign skillfully draws on lies, exaggerations, fictions, partial truths, and other reality distortion techniques to attack the target's character.

A distortion campaign does not intend to help the target. It is inherently destructive. When a truly caring person attempts to help his or her spouse by, for instance, getting them help with a substance abuse or other problem, this is not a distortion campaign, even if the recipient of the attention is angry or even embarrassed about it. This is a result of caring and empathy, not selfishness and cruelty.

Distortion campaigns are often long-term projects begun long before the breakup. They give the perpetrator "justification regarding what she or he has done or is about to do to the target, be it having affairs, kicking them out of the home, filing false domestic violence charges, running away with the children, stealing large quantities of joint money and assets, or some other hostile actions."[28] By the time the target is aware of the distortions, people around her may have been hearing for a long time that she is some evil, horrible person.

The perpetrator is likely to involve many other people in the distortion campaign. Many are passive participants who will listen and believe the lies. Others become actively involved in spreading them further, as in my case. There may, in fact, be dozens of people who have never even met the target, who believe and repeat the lies. I remember visiting a store where Peter was moonlighting after my divorce. He happened to be there as I approached the checkout. I had the boys with me. The female clerk, whom I had never seen, much less met, looked afraid of me! "Good luck," Peter whispered to the clerk as she nervously checked out my items. By this time, I was used to this treatment, but it was the first time I realized how far his campaign had stretched.

Perpetrators tend to pick false accusations that are difficult to prove. Lies in a distortion campaign "revolve around false claims of partner abuse, child abuse, perverse sexual behaviors, drug and

---

[28] "BPD Distortion Campaigns," *www.angiemedia.com*

substance abuse, mental illness, and criminal conduct. The victims of the distortion campaign often are treated as pariahs or even criminals, assumed to be guilty without any evidence whatsoever."[29] The perpetrator gains sympathy and many allies. If the truth becomes known, the situation is usually far past repair. In my case, I had to move on to an entirely new life, and gain new friends to add to the several who supported me. Few friendships remained from the marriage, except for the strong long-time friendships I had brought into it; the friends I had made on my own, mostly from the children's preschool and other activities; and a couple of neighbors.

The kicker about a vilification campaign is that many of the defamatory statements may not be about the target at all, but the perpetrator himself. This behavior is known as "projection."[30] (Many of these tactics are associated with Borderline Personality Disorder and Narcissistic Personality Disorder. Not all perpetrators are Borderline, but these attributes perfectly match the components of such a campaign in a divorce.)

It is shocking how the attackers skillfully manipulate the system and all in it, even their therapists. Let's face it; if they are adept at handling the police, who have the power to make an arrest, there's often little trouble persuading marriage counselors, family friends, and anyone else useful to their side.

---

[29]Ibid.
[30]Ibid.

How a Distortion Campaign Affects the Target

o   She is alienated from her family and friends;

o   She may lose contact with her children for months or even years;

o   She may lose her job;

o   She might have to spend tens of thousands of dollars fighting false accusations;

o   She may have a restraining order placed upon her based on false accusations;

o   She may end up in prison on false accusations;

o   She may develop a severe mental illness, including depression, an anxiety disorder, and post traumatic stress disorder (PTSD);

o   She may commit suicide.

Source: National Institute of Mental Health

8

MAN VERSUS BITCH

"If the police must be called, you call them... Under no circumstances do you ever admit to yelling, threatening, raising your voice, raising your hand, or hitting her and here, I don't care if you lie."
—Divorce Self-Defense 101, www.dumpyourwifenow.com

Steven's Story

"What is ironic here is that, in my opinion, setting up your partner happens exponentially more to men. This is from personal experience. I filed for divorce. For the next six years, my wife launched horrible accusations against me. I am embarrassed to admit that I went to jail too. When I got to court, there was no real trial. I think judges are reluctant to consider the accusations might be false. Mine didn't ask for sufficient evidence against me; he only seemed concerned about being politically correct.

"My children were the biggest victims. Me? Just $10,000 poorer after spending my savings, fruitlessly defending myself. This was money I could have spent on supporting them.

"After six years, I have learned to accept what I have. I even have come to terms with what the children went through. They know what happened. I choose not to have any contact at all with my ex-wife. I don't even talk to her in public. She's always shocked and upset by this. She has never admitted to any wrongdoing; she's never apologized to the children or me. There is no accountability.

"Anyway, I'm sure this happens to mothers, but I believe it happens more to us fathers. I know loving, responsible mothers too are hurt by the courts. What victimizes us, victimizes the children. The first five years following my divorce, I could not believe what I witnessed in courtrooms. It was so surreal, I was dumbfounded. I watched the nightmare developing before my eyes, based on no truth or evidence, and I was powerless to stop it or control the damage.

"I used to believe in the law, and respected all authority without question. Now it is my opinion that the family courts lack ethics, professionalism, and consideration of children's emotions. Our country simply doesn't want to address this. It's like the skeleton in the closet; it's the family secret we're all supposed to ignore.

"That any parent, mom or dad, would be imprisoned over total untruths or maybe even partial-truths, is wrong. You women have my empathy, you do.

"My nightmare continued after the initial custody hearing. My ex remarried. What she didn't tell me was that her new husband had just gotten out of jail. He had a long history of hard drugs and violence. The mother of two of this man's children tracked me down. She broke down and cried, telling me not to let him be around my children. So I requested that the girls live with me full time.

"Once my ex heard I wanted sole custody, she started filing reports out of the blue. She called me a bully, even though I was raising the girls 70 percent of the time. She shoved me one day when I was picking up the girls. She called the police and filed a Protection from Abuse petition (PFA) against me. This was clearly retaliatory; all this happened within a week after I asked for sole custody. I was arrested again. Numerous court appearances and thousands of dollars later, later, I ended up with at about 40 percent custody.

"So, to any human being that this happens to, moms, dads, and especially the children, I would like to put my arm around them and say, 'I'm sorry, very sorry, that this happened to you.' It's wrong. The courts are wrong. It's the reality of our culture."

Steven's story illustrates that women employ this kind of set-up too. These actions are deplorable no matter who pulls them. As Steven points out, the children are the biggest losers.

Fathers' rights groups perpetuate the notion that this happens more to men than women. Without a breakdown of domestic violence arrests by gender, we cannot be sure. Although the laws were originally set up to protect women, the fathers' rights groups allege that this backlash effect stems from women abusing these laws first. Suddenly it became easier to call the police and have an abusive spouse removed. This was the purpose of the law: to remove the abuser before he could do more harm. The swiftness with which a removal could be carried out quickly became, in some instances, a retaliatory act. One sudden phone call can skew a divorce in one's favor, as all our stories reveal. Fathers' rights organizations claim men had no choice but to start using these laws against women, to prevent it from happening to them. This is the "get to the phone first" mentality.

"Shared Parenting" Means Lowered Child Support

Another possible scenario is that when domestic violence moved from the social realm to the criminal—and, therefore, legal—arena, men may have recognized they had a distinct advantage: They usually have more resources to fight. This not only involves money, but support from other men ranging from those in high places, to other fathers who shared the same issues. "Fathers' rights" organizations, which originally emerged in the 1970s, began gaining strength in the 1980s alongside more pro-female legislation, and now ironically wield real power in response to VAWA.

Two pillars of the fathers' rights platform are the concept of "shared parenting," and an intense crusade to lower child support. Shared parenting, or joint custody, is a collaborative agreement in which the care of the children is equal (or at least more equal than a normal primary-custody arrangement, in which the child lives with one parent and has visitation with the other).[31] A shared parenting arrangement between the biological parents follows a plan to which both parents

---

[31] "Shared Parenting Law & Legal Definition." *Legal Definitions Legal Terms Dictionary*. N.p., n.d. Web. 27 June 2011. *http://definitions.uslegal.com/s/shared-parenting/* Author's Note: Many states recognize two forms of joint custody: joint physical custody, and joint legal custody. In joint legal custody, both parents share decisions on education, health, religion, and extracurricular activities. Parents sometimes each choose two of these four areas of the child's life, to be the deciding decision maker if the parents cannot agree. If a parent has primary, or sole, physical custody, the child resides mostly with that parent, and a schedule is agreed upon for staying with the other parent. Thus it is possible to have joint legal custody, but for one parent to have sole physical custody.

agree. While a shared parenting plan does not prohibit child support, the implication is there may be a lesser amount assigned if the child spends time with each parent more equally.

Kim Gandy, former President of the National Organization for Women (NOW) has contended "presumptive joint custody" only furthers the extent to which an abuser can continue to exploit. "It creates an unparalleled opportunity for belligerent former spouses to carry on their personal agendas or vendettas through the children—and with the blessing of the courts," she said in an article by former Michigan NOW President Gloria Woods. "Attorneys often referred to it jokingly as the 'lawyer protection act' because repeated trips to court over minor issues kept the fees rolling in, and the mothers were more likely to suffer."[32]

The fathers' rights movement is arguably the strongest force working against VAWA and related laws designed to protect women. This does not refer to fathers like Steven who fight for custody because they want to protect their children, and who truly believe they will thrive better in their care. This is about a bullying "man versus bitch" mentality, in which the man wants the divorce and all the spoils (or to share fewer of the spoils, whether it is with his ex-wife or his children from the marriage). The fathers' rights organizations claim they simply seek a way to try to get the courts to more evenly consider a custody case, and "not always defer to the mother." They argue that historically, courts did not view each situation in the true best interest of the child.

Regardless of whether or not this is true, the fathers' rights crusade has become a militant movement. In some cases men are

---

[32] Woods, Gloria. "Father's Rights' Groups: Beware Their Real Agenda." NOW, n.d. Web. 27 June 2011. *http://www.now.org/nnt/03-97/father.html*

coached publicly on using malicious tactics to accomplish what seem like sinister goals: to remove or at least significantly reduce their financial obligations to their children, and return to positions of power, not only in their current lives but over their ex-wives.

Author Lundy Bancroft believes the problem is more pernicious than just the existence and influence of the fathers' rights groups. "Abusers are more and more getting fed by these father supremacy organizations, the whole father supremacy movement which calls itself the fathers' rights movement," he told me. "Let's call it what it is."

He goes a step further in typifying these men. "These guys are very, very obvious male supremacists when you read their stuff."

It is easy to find their stuff. Just search the Internet for fathers' rights, divorce tactics (which, even as a generic search, yields mostly websites for men), and the like. Many of these sites appear to be attorney-run.

One of the slickest divorce-oriented sites fueling this industry, *www.brutaldivorcetactics.com*, features a legal "dream team" starring in a 4-DVD set in a "Just for Men" version.

Regardless of whether men or women more often use these ploys against one another, fathers' rights sites foster outrage that women do this. Yet advice for men to pull these same ploys seems to flow freely— sometimes elsewhere on the same sites (where it is then repackaged and promoted as justifiable "self defense").

Aside from the arrest ploy (after which men are sometimes advised to enact orders of protection against their wives and change the locks so their wives cannot return), some common suggestions for men include: cancel all credit cards bearing the wife's name; clean out bank and investment accounts and redirect all deposits to a bank account to which she has no access; quickly become more involved in children's and school activities to get more credit and face time; seize the wife's empty pill bottles and therapy records to cast a shadow on her mental competence, especially her competence as a mother; and remove all valuables, including her own jewelry she might wish to sell or hock, in order to further hinder her ability to pay fees for a competent attorney.

A striking development in the fathers' rights campaign is that women—typically second wives, girlfriends or female family members—are joining the ranks, and even pulling much of the load. Some fathers' rights oriented websites directly appeal to the current woman in the dad's life. By some accounts, it would seem these women do the lion's share of the legwork, attending meetings alone, doing the paperwork, crafting the arguments, and so on.[33] These women, while seeming to be used by this male system, have a stake in the outcome of a child support fight. They commonly contend a man's financial obligations to a former family negatively affect their own relationships and children.

Check out the solicitous female-geared verbiage featured on *www.women4fathersrights.com*: "Now make no mistake, you cannot appear in court for him, but you can fill the paperwork out, you can do the

---

[33] Nazario, Sonia. "The Second Wives' Crusade: Those Men. They Get Married and Start a Family. Then There's That Messy Divorce. They Get Married Again, and the Second Wife Wants What the First Wife Had. See Where We're Headed Here? Los Angeles Times." *Featured Articles From The Los Angeles Times.* 3 Dec. 1995. Web. 27 June 2011. Print.

legwork, you can join our organization... you can definitely be a huge help."[34]

An Organized Attack

According to Dr. Michael Flood, a sociologist at La Trobe University's Australian Research Centre in Sex, Health and Society, the fathers' rights movement spans not only the U.S. but the U.K., Ireland, Canada, New Zealand, and Australia.

"Some fathers' rights groups send misogynist messages, use strategies such as harassment, stalking and intimidation, and strive to chip away at programs and services for women and children," Dawson reported. "They deny the extent of domestic violence and offer sympathy to the perpetrators.

"Since many domestic violence laws just came into effect in the 1990s, it is cause for concern when an organized group sets out to attack them. This group is considered to be strong, organized, and likely, well-funded."[35]

Flood continued: "The fathers' rights groups we should be most afraid of are the seemingly sensible ones. Some FR groups distance themselves from the 'extremists' who make wild, misogynistic claims and threats and adopt tactics of direct action. Instead, these groups concentrate on political lobbying, and they are creating changes in

---

[34] Gac, Dennis. "Women For Fathers Rights." N.p., n.d. Web. 27 June 2011. *http://www.women4fathersrights.com/*

[35] Dawson, Joan M.. "Responsible Parenting and Fathers' Rights: An Interview With Michael Flood." Ohmy News International, n.d. Web. 27 June 2011. *http://www.stopfamilyviolence.org/info/custody-abuse/fathers-rights/responsible-parenting-and-fathers-rights-an-interview-with-michael-flood*

family law. At the same time, their perspectives are still misguided, their influence is dangerous. FR groups have successfully shifted family laws in some jurisdictions so that fathers' contact with children is privileged over children's safety. Children are being forced into contact with fathers who've been violent to them or their mothers.

"FR groups have also encouraged the lie that women routinely make false accusations of child abuse or domestic violence, and the myth that domestic violence is gender-equal."[36]

A few men I spoke with contended that current legislation advocating fair treatment of women actually sets us on even footing with men, instead of existing to protect women. We want to be treated fairly? Then take it like a *man*.

"Just remember, if you're a man, the problem is 'that's just the way the system works,'" said Adam, a single father. "Equality has many burdens and, unfortunately, one of them is fair treatment in a dirty fight.

"The problem is perception. Men are perceived as the more violent sex, but the growth into equality is showing that women are as prone to, and capable of, domestic violence as men. Unfortunately, perceptions are not keeping up with the actual shifts."

He added, "While women have grieved inside the marriage, men rarely see the divorce coming, and when it does, it's a huge shock. One partner is ready to move on, and one has his world turned upside down. This can and sometimes does lead to violence." Adam did not say whether he was a member of a fathers' rights group.

Flood contended the fathers' rights groups as a whole "deny the extent of men's violence against women, excuse or justify this violence,

---

[36] Ibid.

oility with the perpetrators by blaming others

amily law system."

in FR groups have used violence," he said. "To the

groups assume that all fathers accused of domestic

vi   .ild abuse are being accused falsely, they fail to protect

childre. .om harm. As part of encouraging fathers' positive relationships with children, we should be upholding laws and policies addressing domestic violence and child abuse, not trying to undermine them."[37]

"I Didn't See It Coming"

In all the stories in this book, this type of ambush was so unexpected—by design—we just failed to see it coming. We simply did not know you could just pick up the phone and *do* that.

There is a kind of invisible line in the sand between a shaky marriage where there is at least some respect or sense of responsibility to one another remaining, and where war is declared. Anyone in a relationship needs to recognize the erosion of empathy and respect, and protect him or herself if the other party prepares to step over that line.

---

[37] Ibid.

Grace's Story

"I am a non-custodial mother from Michigan. My ex-husband and I have four children together; two are in their early 20s now, and the other two are in their teens. Throughout our 13-year marriage, Mark was controlling, and mentally and physically abusive to the children and me. He continued to abuse the children after our divorce. He is an alcoholic.

"Isolation was one of his methods of abuse. He separated me from all my friends, saying they were bad and making up reasons why. After that, he started barring my family members. The icing on the cake was when he sold our house and all the children's outdoor toys, and said he was going to move us all to Montana in order to seclude me from everyone! He never allowed me to work because some male 'might look at me.'

"I knew I had to get out. I had to make a plan and escape while Mark was away; I was not able to take the children at that moment. I managed to contact my sister, and I fled. By that night, Mark was calling my sister and threatening to put our four children into foster care. My sister told him not to do this, and to please bring the children to her.

"So the next day, my sister and her friends hid me down the street from her home and Mark brought the children. Then he went through my sister's house tearing everything apart looking for me, but of course I was not there to be found.

"I summoned the police just once after we were separated, because Mark would not stop stalking me and showing up where the children and I were living. He appeared on my door step and burst through the door. Then he ripped the phone out of the wall so that I would not be able to call the police. He stole my car. The police issued a warrant for his arrest, but they never followed through.

"Mark continued to stalk me at my job. I finally had a nervous breakdown. My doctor made me go into hiding, and I had to take a leave of absence from my job for over a month.

"I had the children for 11 years as a single mom. But Mark was always dragging me into court for lies just so he could harass me. He always tried to bribe the children with money to get them to come live with him. They always told him no.

"My now 22-year-old was born with mild cerebral palsy, so he was in and out of the hospitals the first two years of his life. He also had to have orthotic braces, special shoes, and a lot of occupational and physical therapy. I had to drive to Detroit for speech therapy three times a week when he was 7, because no one here offered it. Of course, Mark never went with me; he thought we should just leave my son as he was. So my mother went with me instead.

"All three of my other children suffered from serious hereditary allergies. My now 18-year-old also had an immune deficiency syndrome that affects the mucosal system. He missed many days of school, which all were excused by doctor. I had a home school tutor who came in if he got really sick. Meanwhile, I learned the house I was renting had mold in the basement, and my landlord did nothing to fix this problem.

"So I began working with a realtor and a mortgage company to buy a home for us. I was juggling work and the four boys as I packed to move. So packed boxes were stacked up around the house.

"While the son who had the immune problems was waiting to have sinus surgery, he had a PICC line, a sort of catheter for intravenous fluids, in his arm for about two months. He had to stay home so a nurse could come out and run his IV.

"Well, even though we were homeschooling through that time, the school called the truancy officer on me. When the officer came to the door, he asked about the boxes. I told him I was planning on moving because of the mold in the house.

"Mark must have found out about this because the next day, an ex parte (a judicial proceeding that is conducted for the benefit of one party) was filed on me. Mark used a two-week vacation I had taken with my kids *six years before* to visit my best friend and their godmother in Georgia, as his reason to file. He claimed the boxes I had packed meant I was going to run!

"'Run from what?' I asked. I was always on the board of the PTA at my children's schools, and was very involved with their sports, and every aspect of their lives. Mark never came to their sports or conferences.

"Yet Mark wrote the court and claimed I had once taken the kids and moved out of state—an outrageous lie—and had this documented into our file at the Friends of the Court (FOC) office.

"We went to court. I had my papers from the doctors, and the papers from the realtor and the woman from the mortgage company. The judge would not look at any of it; she just shoved it back to my attorney. The judge proceeded to call me a 'doctor shopper' (although my children had retained the same doctors for over seven years). She inappropriately, not to mention incorrectly, 'diagnosed' me with Munchausen syndrome by proxy, which is a form of child abuse in which a parent induces real or apparent symptoms of a disease in a child. The judge ordered no tests, nor examined their medical histories. She just proclaimed it.

"That is how Mark ended up with custody of our four children. I went into counseling after Mark took them. The bizarre thing was, the family court judge who ultimately gave him custody is on the board of that counseling facility. How ironic is that, when that judge's actions landed me there?

"At that time I lost custody of my children, I was laid off and had no money. The court ordered me to pay child support. When I got back on my feet, I paid the required amount faithfully for years.

"Then one day, Mark had me arrested for back child support. I owed $800 because of that arrearage I accrued from being laid off, back in the beginning. I was incarcerated for about three hours. My mother came to bail me out.

"I was devastated. I had never been arrested. I had never committed any crime in my life! It was degrading and humiliating—obviously what Mark wanted. They patted me down and treated me with complete disrespect. I owed less than $1,000, after all that time paying. How many men owe hundreds of thousands of dollars?

"What they did to me was unbelievable. The judge also suspended my driver's license. Now ask yourself: If the court wants you to pay child support, how are you supposed to pay when you can no longer drive yourself to work? That has got to be the most ridiculous thing I have ever heard.

"I lost more than 10 years with my children because he took them. Those are years I will never get back and all out of spite, control and jealousy."

The Fathers' Rights Movement

Supporters of the fathers' rights movement contend that it is mostly women who make false claims of domestic violence or child abuse in order to gain an upper hand in a divorce or custody dispute. The fathers' rights leaders charge these women aim to prevent fathers from seeing their children.

Fathers' rights groups state that false claims of domestic violence and child abuse are encouraged by the inflammatory "win or lose" nature of child custody hearings, that the police and courts presume men are immediately guilty.

Meanwhile, attorneys and advocates for abused women say that family court proceedings are commonly accompanied by allegations of domestic violence because that is what is happening. Most allegations are not false, they say. They also assert that domestic violence often begins or increases around the time of divorce or separation, something many women in this book saw firsthand.

Fathers' rights members claim to be advocating solid relationships with their children, but in some instances, their focus appears to be the issues they face as divorced or divorcing men, not as fathers. It would seem a man who wants what is best for his children would not rally to lower child support without regard to need, and would not seek to financially cripple the children's mother.

Members of the fathers' rights movement and fathers' rights activists like to emphasize women's role in the movement. The women who join these men often are new partners, second wives, or other family members. Some members even include noncustodial mothers.

According to Dr. Michael Flood: "Many FR groups offer hateful and misogynist stereotypes of women and mothers. FR groups do little to heal the anger and blame felt by many separated fathers. And FR groups in general circulate highly inaccurate and hostile parodies of feminism. Some FR groups use 'softer' and more 'reasonable' rhetoric, but few if any are dedicated to building constructive relationships between separated fathers, mothers, and children."[38]

Flood opined these groups might, in fact, be classified as hate groups. "Negative and hostile depictions of women in general and single mothers in particular are the bread and butter of fathers' rights discourse," he reported. "...Fathers' rights literature routinely depicts women as parasitical, mendacious, and vindictive. First, resident mothers are portrayed as living lives of luxury relative to nonresident fathers, lazy 'sofa loafers' and 'gold-diggers' who are comfortable on government pensions and financially exploiting their ex-partners. As Winchester (1999: 93) found in her interviews with members of the Newcastle branch of the Lone Fathers' Association, group members consistently overestimated single mothers' financial well-being, underestimated the costs and expenses of caring for resident children, and undervalued their ex-partners' domestic work. In fact, a recent analysis of those involved in the child support system found that while nonresident fathers are poor, resident mothers are even poorer, with 75 percent living on incomes below $15,600 per annum (Silvey and Birrell 2004: 50).

"Second, mothers are portrayed as dishonest and vindictive, prone to making false allegations of domestic violence or child abuse and

---

[38] Dawson, Joan M. "Responsible Parenting and Fathers' Rights: An Interview With Michael Flood."

arbitrarily and unilaterally denying nonresident fathers' contact with children... Members of fathers' rights groups also portray their ex-partners as 'tramps,' 'whores,' 'sluts,' 'bitches' and 'adulterers'."[39]

---

[39] Ibid.

9

THE NATURE OF THE ANGER

"A therapist will tell you that depression is anger turned inward. The opposite is also true."—Kelly White[40]

The "Arresting Developments" study noted one reason a female victim might get angry or vocal at the scene is that she feels safe and finally can express her anger at the suspect and system for failing to protect her. "Such outbursts in the presence of police may only serve to slant the view of circumstances in favor of the male suspect, who may deal with the officers in a calm and deliberative manner," the researchers reported.[41]

Jessica described being extremely angry during her fray with her ex-husband, in which he contemptuously announced his decision to divorce her, then flicked his attorney's business card in her face.

It is unsurprising that she was a wreck by the time police caught up with her on her friend's front lawn, and arrested *her* for assault.

---

[40] White, Kelly. *A Safe Place for Women: Surviving Domestic Abuse and Creating a Successful Future*. Alameda, Calif: Hunter House, 2010: 140. Print.
[41] DeLeon-Granados, et al.

Every woman in this book was angry on the night of her arrest—and if she wasn't angry before, she most likely was by the booking process. These set-ups count on the victim being angry so she can successfully be incited, and so the spouse gets the result he wants.

"Anger" seems a dirty word when spoken on many counselors' couches. Anger seems to get the blame for many problems. "Paula, you should not have gotten angry," a therapist might admonish. Never mind that Paula threw that crystal vase at the wall because she had just come across some racy cyber-correspondence between her husband and a female coworker, after months of his denying it and calling her crazy.

Why were we all so angry that we lost control? How did we generally normally functioning women turn into these furious people? This is not to pass the buck or blame our states of mind on others; but anger has an origin. Perhaps it is a reaction to the accumulation of years of some form of abuse, by the spouse or someone else. It could be mountains of pain, frustration, and helplessness piled up over time. Whatever the source of the anger, it is sad that a woman in most instances probably cannot believably call 9-1-1 and report she feels she is being incited into an argument and growing angry, and win the police to her side. Even if she is rightfully angry, and her partner is inciting the argument in an attempt to propogate the abuse while she is in police custody, police likely will interpret her anger as aggressive and threatening because that is what it will look like upon their arrival. In these zero tolerance times, it is she who will go in.

At present, the only way around this, as legal and police sources attest, is to find a way to hold even natural emotions in check.

Anger Understood

The police do not have time to conduct a thorough investigation when they respond to a call. Therapists do—hours of it. Yet anger is often teased out of context and treated like a problem on its own. Certainly, angry people need to work on their anger. It is undeniably dangerous and destructive. But why don't more therapists ask the calm, confident guy sitting next to the angry woman if he might have anything to do with it?

As shown in How To Spot a Set-Up and What To Do, an examination of the sources of our anger long ago could have kept at least some of us out of jail. The skilled therapists are terrific; the best can transform your life. But the mediocre ones can waste your time and money (and sometimes their court-ordered notes can sway a judge).

Just as in choosing an attorney, a doctor, or other professional that will have direct impact on your life, choosing the right therapist to guide you in your self-exploration is critical. Sometimes, just as in getting a second opinion, one has to make many inquiries and shop around.

Other tools to help in a quest for self-discovery include discussing issues with friends; consulting other community resources, such as religious and support groups; reading books on the subjects at hand; and journaling. (Please see additional resources in Appendix C.)

Elizabeth's Story

"I had been supporting my husband Barry while he completed a second degree. We were both in our late 40s and lived in Illinois. Once he earned the degree, he went back to work full time, but somehow we fell into the bad practice of him still not contributing to the household budget.

"I still carried the entire load. I became responsible for the house we lived in, which I had bought before the marriage; insurance; vacation costs; daycare; groceries; and everything else. Barry's paycheck paid for his new car and the mortgage on the house he vacated when we got married. Every weekend, Barry would go to work on that house for a few hours, while contributing little to the care and maintenance of the house we lived in. I actually mowed the lawn the day before I delivered each of my three children. After mowing the lawn one too many times, I cracked down on him, and at least he began paying for child care.

"When the economy collapsed, I lost 80 percent of my consulting business in one year. Yet I was still paying for everything we needed. I was starting to feel resentful when Barry would arrive home with a Starbucks cup in hand, while I had spent hours that week clipping coupons after the children went to bed.

"During this time, I watched my mother's health rapidly deteriorate, and I suggested to Barry that we should seize the opportunity to visit his mother, who lived out of the country. I worried that it would become too late and that we would regret not making the trip.

"My business was such that I now had plenty of time for a trip, if not the money. I had accumulated enough frequent flier miles from credit card purchases over the years to get three free tickets for the children and me. Barry agreed to purchase his ticket on his own.

"Two weeks before we were scheduled to leave, he still had not purchased that ticket. Finally, I caved in and gave him my credit card to buy a ticket before it was too late. A day passed, and he still had not bought it. That evening, I went online and found a fare for $700. I went into the living room where Barry was watching TV and asked him if he would come look at the ticket rate, so that we could go ahead and book the flight.

"'I'm too tired,' he said. 'I'll look at it tomorrow.' As happens in the airline world, 24 hours later, the $700 fare had increased to $1,300. I got upset and pointed this out to Barry. 'Who cares at this point?' he said. 'It's only another $600.'

"After all I'd been through, I most certainly cared. 'I've had enough!' I cried. 'I'm sick of being an enabler, and you need to leave the house.' More words flew back and forth.

"Barry shoved me against a wall, but I got myself together and collected the kids, who needed me to take them to a birthday party. 'I don't want you here when I come back,' I told Barry.

"He had shoved me before, but it was never too severe, including that day. Once he threw a bookend behind my head when I was pregnant. It tore a hole in the wall. He later patched it up and drew a smiley face over it. This is the kind of thing he does when he pretends his actions can be forgotten.

"When the children and I returned to the house three hours later, Barry was still in the house. I told him to leave. He just turned his back toward me. I was incensed. 'Turn around and look at me!' I shouted. I tapped him hard on the shoulder, and he spun around and grabbed my wrist. Trying to disengage from his grasp, I scratched his forearm.

"'You're out of control,' he told me. 'I'm going to call the police.'

"He did; he dialed 9-1-1. All this was going on in my children's presence—it seriously shook them up. When the police arrived, the scratches on Barry's fair skin showed; the bruises on my chest and wrists had yet to appear. The police handcuffed me and put me in the squad car. This, on the day I was supposed to be making cupcakes for my son's birthday the following day. I surely wished I had called 9-1-1 myself.

"One of the most disturbing parts of my arrest was the undisguised scorn of the female officer who booked me into jail. She kept rudely interrupting me as I tried to answer her questions. She fed in distorted information. 'I've had it, and I just want my husband out of my house,' I told her.

"'This is not your house. You're married,' she retorted. 'It's joint marital property.'

"I explained that the house was a premarital asset, and Barry had never contributed to the costs or maintenance of it. 'It's still his,' she said with a shrug. She was clueless about what I owned and what I did not. But her attitude was extremely demeaning, despite its ignorance. When she saw me later, she said, 'Hey lady, I interviewed your kids, and they heard every word of that fight. Don't you even care about that?' I told her that yes, that is why I wanted Barry to leave.

"'My husband should have created peace for the children, instead of treating me disrespectfully again and again in front of them!' I told her, my temper flaring. 'I want the fighting to stop. Their lives shouldn't be like this.'

"She just snorted and shook her head. It was deplorable. One would expect compassion and understanding from a fellow working woman. But she, like the system, was treating me like some kind of animal.

"I was only held at the jail for a few hours, but the arrest made me physically sick. I felt as if I were in a dream, or a lousy made-for-TV movie. The unfairness, the feeling of being the one victimized yet punished, was tough to take. It was the second worst day of my life; the worst was the day my first son, who suffered from seizures as an infant, died.

"I filed for divorce the day the court dropped the charges against me. Barry and I had been married for 10 years. We had tried to patch things up, but the patterns kept repeating themselves. During this time, in counseling, Barry even blew up in front of the therapist once. He opened the door to the waiting room and started yelling to our kids that the marriage was over. After calming him down and finishing the session, the therapist took me aside and said I needed to take care of my kids and leave him. My divorce case is in the court system now.

"I have photographs of the bruises Barry caused on me, so my arrest won't affect my divorce case. The incident did, however, cause me professional damage. My business is one built on reputation, on my name, and the local paper recorded my arrest. We live in a small town where people have long memories. That one 9-1-1 call wiped out decades of volunteer work and professional accomplishments. I was not given the ink to explain my side of the story.

"It turns my stomach to see the local newspaper running mug shots from the suburbs in their paper. It has altered my perception when

I see things like police logs in the paper. 'Guilty until proven innocent' rings true for me.

"I am sure my children and I will feel the financial—and emotional—impact of that horrible 9-1-1 call for years to come."

10

HELP, HOPE, AND HEALING

Gina's Story

"No weapon that is formed against thee shall prosper; and every tongue that shall rise against thee in judgment thou shalt condemn." —Isaiah 54:17

"When this happened to me, I was in my early 20s working as an international flight attendant for a major airline. Prior to that, I had worked as a writer for major TV news stations in a prominent market. So, no, I wasn't an abusive putz with a shady background, but an educated woman with a productive professional life. Today I am self employed as a writer. I enjoy my leadership role in the business world as an African American woman.

"My son's father and I had had a horrible relationship for the two years we had been together. I was afraid to flee because I thought he would kill me. But before my son was born, I gathered my courage and told his father I planned to leave the state with the baby. One day, on the way to the bookstore, he told me he wanted me to sign papers saying I would never take the child and leave. I, of course, refused. He grabbed me by the wrist and threatened me. I pulled away. He grabbed me again. I began to fight him off. The more I fought, the more he resisted. By this time, his shirt was ripped and he had a few scratches on his arm and neck.

"He pulled into a police station parking lot, where an officer saw us arguing. I was arrested on the spot, with my six-month-old son strapped into the car seat in the back of the truck. I remained in jail for one week. One of the most unfair things about this is, he always threatened to call the police if I didn't do what he wanted. I'd summoned the police myself before out of fear of him, and they always looked at me like I was the criminal. He was never arrested.

"My record was not expunged because this happened four times over a two-year period. I absolutely despise cops. Mostly, I have no faith in our legal system. To see the way my son's father and the cops would look at each other in the courtroom and smirk, as if they were in on some secret, while I was sitting there with my life in the balance, wondering what would happen to my child if I were locked away, made my stomach turn.

"He even threatened to fax my bosses when I was at the airlines, telling them about my arrests. I had to sit down with the top brass and explain the situation. This worked for me. It is also worth noting that I held three other jobs after I left the airlines—I told them all about my record, and they hired me despite that. I am now self-employed by choice, because I wanted to craft my life according to my desires. It's about lifestyle more than money (believe me—it's all about lifestyle!).

"I haven't lost all faith in men, and I know there are some very good ones out there, but I will absolutely never trust my son's father again. Today, I keep all communications very brief and only via email, if possible (he shares custody of our son).

"I will never, ever trust that he has honest, good intentions toward me. He continues, to this day, to taunt me and boast that I, not he, have a police record. I get sick of heads turning and eyebrows raising every time I share my story. Even though I'm a very petite woman, people look at me like I surely must be some savage beast.

"He's even using it now as fodder to fight for custody of our son, who is now 11. I'm not worried about that. My son and I are close and he has expressed no desire to live with his dad. The solicitor general for the county and my defense attorney understood he was trying to set the stage to get custody of our son; as my defense attorney said to me, 'He set you up real good.'

"I am at a point, more than 10 years after the arrests, where I own what happened as part of my story. It has informed who I am and what I do. It's not something to run or hide from. It's something I can talk about openly, honestly, and freely. It no longer owns me or has any power over me. Reaching this point did not come easily, but I'm here, and it's perfectly okay.

"So that I can give other women hope, I want to stress that back when I was afraid to leave, afraid this man would kill me, I became incredibly depressed. I thought I was ugly—utterly undesirable—and I lived for about five years like a zombie. I felt dead inside. I prayed for five straight years for God to resolve that situation.

"Today (four years after I left him, 11 years since the arrests), I am happy and vibrant, and absolutely confident this is my best life (cue *Oprah* soundtrack!). My son and I take trips together, hang out together (he's my "road dog"), and enjoy our life together. My son sees his dad every other weekend.

"Oh, and I'm single by choice. That is major, because a part of me stayed so long because I didn't think anyone else would want me. Now I know better. As the old Negro spiritual says, 'I wouldn't take nothing for my journey now.'"

T his book has been intended not only to inform and caution, but to provide multiple examples of eyewitness testimony that some policy reform and radically improved law enforcement training are desperately needed to curb these destructive trends. Policy makers need to refocus on looking after the real victims, whether they are male or female, adult or child.

It seems almost too much of a dichotomy to counsel women to protect themselves from someone who is supposed to be protecting *them*. To go from trying 100 percent to make the marriage work, to having to prepare for battle in the form of a contentious divorce sounds impossible and crazy. But these days, especially with the laws and court system we have to work with, women must find a way to strike this balance.

It becomes even harder if, as in Jessica's and Gina's cases, women are constantly told that they are defective. As Jessica puts it, "I drank the Kool-Aid. I thought there was something wrong with me. No one else would ever want me."

Women who identify with this treatment, who feel unworthy of love and care, need to examine why they feel this way. As soon as they realize they are in dangerous alliances, they must immediately seek domestic violence services.

Women's shelters offer support, legal advice, guidance, and counseling. Women also can consult family, friends, therapists, their religious or cultural communities, or any other resources at hand. They must determine if they are the victims of abuse; abused women often have no idea they could fall under such a label. They must seek help right away.

If the marriage seems to be heading for divorce, this is critical. Domestic violence experts caution that abusers ramp it up when the victim tries to leave.[42] Even if she manages to leave safely, an abusive ex can try to punish her in court—as illustrated throughout this book, to use the law against her to gain advantage in court and punish her further.

If a partner wants to leave, a woman cannot afford to go into denial and pretend nothing is wrong. Trying to "win him back" if he is out the door rarely works. This is not to say there are not inspiring instances of couples working it out, and reuniting. This is also not to imply that anyone, male or female, seeking a divorce will resort to set-up tactics. Not every person who wants a divorce, or whose spouse wants one, wants to destroy the other person. It would be a beautiful thing if all divorcing couples would seek to preserve civility and respect on behalf of their children, if not each other.

However, some women, fearing their partner will leave or is dissatisfied, will "double up" and try to do the work for both of them. Not only is it unhealthy to do this, it is dangerous. Our society is a litigious one, and lawyers are trained to provide their clients every possible advantage. Unfortunately, laws such as these aggressive arrest policies are easily manipulated to offer such advantages.

---

[42] White, *A Safe Place for Women*, 92.

Anyone facing a divorce needs to get savvy to the signs of a set-up. This does not mean there will be one. But it is imperative to be on guard. When divorce enters the picture, the rules change, and they change fast. We are all here to say, it can catch you by surprise.

Tracing the Pattern

Even if a woman is not the victim of physical or other overt abuse, she needs to carefully consider the patterns in the marriage and determine if her spouse has taken advantage of her in the past—in any way. For instance, financially. Has he always controlled the purse strings? Has he kept vital information from her? Does he make all the financial and other decisions, without regard to her desires and needs?

Such a person who feels himself entitled, who treats his wife as other than an equal, will likely use every tool he has to annihilate her in a divorce.

The best way to protect yourself, your life, and your children's lives is to recognize abuse for what it is—and know who you are dealing with.

Agents of Change

Groups like Survivors in Action exist to promote domestic violence reform—going beyond what Alexis Moore of Survivors in Action (*www.survivorsinaction.org*) calls "traditional awareness" to a new awareness of key issues.

"Many family law and civil attorneys are not prepared to address these issues, so we must address them through awareness programs that are centered around this topic," said Moore. "This is part of DV reform. The awareness programs of yesterday for domestic violence are not working to address the issues that are important, like this one."

One of Moore's key issues is redistributing the power in domestic violence organizations. "We have billions in funding not being utilized to assist victims," she contended. "Instead, it is spent on programs that are not helping anyone other than those who work at these agencies. We need DV survivors on the board of directors at the Federal, state and local levels and include them in the process of ensuring 'no victim left behind.'"

Moore claims she has asked to join the Department of Justice VAWA committee, where the laws are created and victim services established, for five years, but that her efforts so far have been unsuccessful.

"Federal and state DV coalitions and partnerships, and the county DV organizations as well, need to be held accountable for every dime they spend," she said. "When victims are left behind, they need a place to turn to report their experiences so the funding does not continue to go to organizations that are not taking care of them."

For instance, the National Center for Victims of Crime has cut its hotline because of lack of funding. They currently offer training only and no longer call themselves a "victim resource center." This includes the hotline for the National Stalking Resource Center, also closed.[43]

---

[43] "Victim Assistance." *National Center for Victims of Crime.* Web. 20 Feburary 2012. *http://ncvc.org/ncvc/Main.aspx*

Advocates for domestic violence reform suggest more funding needs to go to lawyers who can provide hands on assistance to victims who need their records expunged, and other legal aid.

"Survivors In Action and many other organizations are ready, willing, and able to do the job and to do the heavy lifting and, most importantly, put the needs of victims first," said Moore. "But we cannot do this without being placed in a position of leadership, and given the resources to take action."

❧

Despite the strain of dealing with getting my criminal charges dropped and minding all the P's and Q's and jumping through all the hoops, when all was said and done, I honestly do not feel the charges affected the overall outcome. I do believe I had to work 1,000 times harder in my divorce than Peter to ensure this, and that having an excellent attorney made all the difference. Still, it can be done. I had top-notch, proactive representation, and I imperfectly yet earnestly tried to follow the rules as well as I could.

Bottom line, I went from just about every strike in the book against me, to triumphing, as I measured it. I went from hoping I would at least get joint custody, to getting primary physical custody. I was also given the option to stay in our house so my boys and I would not have to move.

During mediation, I began to realize Peter's worst fear was being cut off entirely. I had no intention of trying to keep the children from him. He was a generally conscientious dad. At the same time, I realized I would need after-school child care since I would need to return to work full time. Peter worked from home.

I had an idea. I shared it with my attorney, and we suggested that the boys could be with Peter every afternoon after school, if he wished. Because of this agreement, the boys would not need aftercare from school and get to spend extra time with their dad. Peter eased up. It was almost like magic. It was undeniably a win-win-win-win situation.

My divorce case did not go to trial; it was settled in mediation before the court date. I received the most child support the law and Peter's financial situation allowed me (the guidelines have since become stricter and trickier in Georgia—another reason to insist on the best representation). I received one year of alimony, not a large sum, but it helped. Peter and I split the debt. That was tough, especially since I did not even have a full time job at the time, but I held on to my most precious assets: my children.

Not long after the divorce was final, I was offered the full-time job I had been campaigning for at the health center. It offered me a certain amount of built-in child care, so that I did not have to feel I was separated from my children for long periods. They could go enjoy the play center, which along with toys was outfitted with "big kid" computers and board games, while I taught swim lessons.

The job did require me to work weekends, which was OK for a while, but soon I realized not a day went by when I was not called in to go check something or solve a problem. Peter even offered me his court-decreed alternating Sunday evenings for a while because he saw I was losing valuable time with the boys. I found another full-time job that offered better pay and a more clearly defined schedule.

One of the most surprising aspects of the divorce was, Peter and I realized we agreed on most details of the boys' lives. We have worked together quite a lot, hard as it may be to believe, given our history. The boys even tell their peers their parents "are friends."

We still live in the same metro area as Peter, and the boys see him regularly. We collaborate a great deal with all the coming and going as the boys grow older and have more activities. Now I am home-based once again, as a writer and small business owner, and my sons are home with me most afternoons.

I have remarried. Three-year-old twins balance our family and create delightful chaos at all times. Both are adept at picking locks and climbing to dizzying heights in seconds. One is a girl.

We moved from the suburbs out to the country, where nights are dark and quiet. The children and our dog can run free. We have acquired two rabbits and a flock of lovely egg-laying chickens. The schools are first-rate and offer many options.

My best advice? No matter what is happening, strive to be fair in your divorce, and do what is best for your children. Sometimes I think these stringent divorce tactics are launched because it is what the other side expects *you* to do, as well. I can see that a lot of Peter's behavior during the divorce was acting out from high emotionality—it was his second divorce—and militant counsel that brought out his worst and fed on his anger. Once the custody arrangement began to work, much of the animosity dissipated.

Then, there is nothing to do but put one foot firmly in front of the other and do not look behind you, nor too far ahead. As Jesus said:

"Therefore do not worry about tomorrow, for tomorrow will worry about itself." (Matthew 6:34)

EPILOGUE

A Memory

After my divorce was final, the boys and I basked in the serenity that descended over the house after all the marital strife was gone. One of my favorite memories, however, is a night I spent alone.

I sat in my freshly painted downstairs master bedroom, the same one in which I was interrogated by the police that awful evening, the same room in which I used to lock myself every night.

The boys were spending the night with their dad. For a while after the divorce, those nights alone felt strange, stressful, and sad. I was getting used to it, though, and learning to enjoy the downtime after the demanding one-parent 24-hour supervision that comes with divorce.

The stereo system had gone with Peter, but I still had my little portable boom box. It was dusk. The windows were half open, and a warm-weather breeze ruffled my toile curtains. The crickets chimed in with Nickel Creek's fiddling. An aromatherapy candle the boys and I had made—one of our craft store projects—flickered on my nightstand. I felt rested. I did not need a makeshift "office" anymore. I was still part-time at the fitness center but trying out for the full-time job there. I even had a date with a spectacularly handsome man the following night.

And I felt peace.

Editorial Note: The insights provided by the experts in this section are not meant to constitute legal or other advice or counsel. They are guidelines to help the reader be aware of current trends in legal, law enforcement, and domestic realms. The only legal advice given is to hire a lawyer of your own choosing to answer questions related to your particular situation.

HOW TO SPOT A SET-UP AND WHAT TO DO

"The abuser's problem is not that he responds inappropriately to conflict. His abusiveness is operating prior to the conflict: it usually creates the conflict, and it determines the shape the conflict takes." —Lundy Bancroft[44]

I t seems inconceivable to shift from the enormous leap of faith of "'til death do us part" and "making the marriage work" to "being on guard against a divorce set-up." Indeed, the difficulty of this is, it is hard to discern where a partner stops working on the marriage and starts plotting a divorce and jockeying for position.

How do you play both sides?

First, you must bring yourself to recognize the signs, because they will be there. Usually a partner will not start with the emergency 9-1-1 call; there will often have been something brewing for some time.

---

[44] Bancroft, Lundy. *Why Does He Do That? Inside the Minds of Angry and Controlling Men.* New York: Putnam's Sons, 2002: 140. Print.

Tip-Offs

As in the stories of women in this book, there are several primary ways a person might use a 9-1-1 call. It can be an out and out divorce set-up, to gain advantage from the get-go (which can be precipitated by legal and "community" coaching from other people or groups). It can be a way to have an ace in the hole to produce in case his wife wants to leave him (as in Ashley's husband's "forbidding" her to have her record expunged in case he wanted to use it). It can occur when there is already an abusive situation, as in Elizabeth's case, and the husband wants to deflect the blame onto his wife. It can be a capricious call quickly spun into an opportunity. And it can be an act of vengeance, to punish or control.

Consider if any of these factors is going on (other tip-offs for behavior and attitude can be found in the Practical Protection section):

o Your husband is abusive, physically, emotionally, financially or otherwise. Spot the common theme in many stories in this book: Some women had been shoved and otherwise abused by their partners. The victims knew in the backs of their minds that their partners' actions were abusive.

o You know your marriage is building to a divorce.

o Your instincts tell you something is up. Trust them. It is painful to contemplate the life, the marriage, the family, you have worked so hard to build might be threatened. Look at it this way: Being careful is not harmful; if your marriage is strained but salvageable, taking precautions will not hurt it.

Here are other essential and easy to implement ideas you can use to protect yourself: legally, financially, practically, and even spiritually.

Legal Protection

Randy Kessler, founding partner of Kessler and Solomiany, LLC (*www.ksfamilylaw.com*), represents celebrities, sports stars, and other public figures (and "real" people too). He is Chair of the Family Law Section of the American Bar Association (2011-2012) and teaches family law at Atlanta's John Marshall Law School. His legal commentary has been featured on news outlets including ABC and CNN News, *USA Today, Newsweek, The Wall Street Journal, The New York Times, The Atlanta Journal-Constitution, The Today Show, Anderson Cooper 360,* ESPN, *People, Cosmopolitan, Time, Dr. Phil, Nancy Grace, Jane Velez Mitchell, In Session,* and *Prime News.* He also has extensive experience helping victims of these kinds of traps.

Here are Kessler's best legal insights for potentially avoiding them, or at least keeping yourself in the best possible light:

o Pretend there is a judge standing next to you at all times. "These days, you never know if someone is recording you and filming you. Anything you do can be used against you," Kessler says. That invisible judge will help you hold yourself in check, and monitor your own behavior and reactions.

o Carry a tape recorder. There are two ways to use it. You can pull it out and show that you've got it, which will eliminate some violence.

Or, you can use it to record him for use later. Tape recording laws differ from state to state. Some require you to inform the other person you are recording him; if not, it is illegal, and therefore inadmissible. (Author's Note: As a reporter, I had to get my sources' confirmation on tape, for the record. This, obviously, would not work if you want to record your partner secretly. To find out your state's laws, visit this website: *http://www.rcfp.org/taping/states.html*)

○ One of the best things you can do, according to Kessler, is to have a witness. If you sense that a bad situation might arise, have a friend on call, on speed dial, who can come over on a moment's notice. Or get out. If the situation warrants, never mind if he can use this against you. "You leave because it is the safe thing to do," Kessler says. "You can justify it honestly."

○ The truth is, beyond monitoring the signs, nothing is going to stop a 9-1-1 call from being made. People have even injured themselves and claimed the spouse inflicted the wound. But you have your own weapon with you at all times: You can be prepared. Be cool. If you are the calm one, the police are going to talk to you. The cops can do two things—they can report what someone tells them happened, or they can describe what they saw. If they see you acting crazy, they can tell the judge. "Then it becomes an eyewitness record," Kessler points out. "That kind of evidence can be used against a person in a trial."

○ Get a divorce attorney. A good one. Do your homework. Have him or her at the ready. (Just because you have a divorce lawyer, does not mean you have to get a divorce.) Kessler says, "If your spouse is one of these guys or gals who could pull this, you've got to be ready." If you do not know of an attorney firsthand, call the state and local bar organizations to start. "Search online," Kessler suggests. "Ask women's shelters for referrals, or ask your church community or other religious support groups. Those are good starts."

(Author's Note: Also, pay attention to who the players are in complicated divorces you know about. If an attorney represents someone admirably, put him or her on your list.

I first consulted the female attorney who was representing all my friends at the fitness center. By the time I reached my jail story, her eyes had glazed over. She didn't get it; it was over her head. Next.

On a strong referral, I contacted another female attorney, from a high-profile Atlanta firm, who had a very tough reputation and seemed very exacting about what she wanted from my behavior—recording every conversation with my spouse, and the like. She had a scheduled surgery that would delay her getting on my case by about two weeks. I needed someone yesterday. Next.

Then my lifelong friend Kimberly reminded me of the attorney who represented her husband in his custody case and did a great job. I called him up. He instantly understood the drill and quoted me his retainer fee. I could not have made a better choice. He wrapped up my complicated case and tied up every loose end with what I now recognize as dizzying speed for any divorce.)

o   You must get out and get away if an incident starts. If you cannot, sequester yourself in a safe place in your home and call police. Each situation is different, but the key is *staying safe*. Kessler suggests that if you do feel you must leave the premises, you can write down everything that happened in detail afterwards. When you're trying to remember it six months later in court, your memory can be challenged. But if you can point to a written document, this is much more credible.

o A vast majority of the time, women are not convicted, many lawyers say. The prosecution dismisses the case. You can take solace in this. You have got to see that light at the end of the tunnel. Innocent people are rarely convicted in our society. "That's the beauty of our system," Kessler says. "It's hard to be convicted if you're innocent. If you didn't do anything, there is reasonable doubt. The burden of proof is harder."

o Be aware of outside indicators that something might be happening. "Listen to your friends," Kessler stresses. "Their emotions do not taint their objectivity." You love your spouse. But your friends and family have your best interests at heart. Recall comments they may have made in the past, and bring up the subject with them. Ask them outright what they think about what is going on.

Why Does a Scratch Trump a Bruise?

When we began comparing notes, Jessica and I often pondered: When police arrive, why does a scratch trump a bruise? Why did our arresting officers focus on minor scratches, as bruises were already appearing on our arms and legs?

Kessler surmises that while a bruise can come about in a variety of situations or accidents, a scratch may appear as more intentional, more aggressive, to police.

"It is probably easier to tell that the scratch is fresh," he says. "A bruise can occur anytime, and can happen in any number of ways." It is a fact that bruises can take a while to bloom, and in the police' haste to wrap up the investigation, a scratch might be all the physical evidence they have.

It is essential to take photographs of bruises and any other injuries as soon as possible to give your attorney and produce at your trial.

Police Protection

Steve Kardian (*www.stevekardian.com*) is retired after 30 years of police work in the New York area. Now a security and safety expert, he runs a very successful women's self defense program and lectures widely. He has become one of the nation's go-to experts on women's safety, crime prevention and risk reduction, appearing on *Inside Edition*, CNN, *Fox News*, *The Morning Show*, CBS, NBC, *Men's Journal*, *The New York Times*, *Woman's Day*, *Best Life Magazine*, *USA Today*, *The Wall Street Journal*, and *Sports Illustrated*.

Here are Kardian's best insights for protecting yourself. As always, the best protection is that ounce of prevention.

o   The minute things go bad, and the situation is beyond resolution, notify police. Wait for them to arrive and then be as truthful and honest as you possibly can. The laws are set up to protect *you*. In many cases in this book, women did not avail themselves of this protection, choosing to "go it alone." And then their partners turned the tables.

o   Women must learn to recognize and identify a dangerous situation, Kardian stresses. Are you seeing odd signs? Is your partner acting strangely?

o   Tell the truth—your whole truth. (Author's Note: Kardian explained that my lunging for the cell phone, which was Peter's personal property, appeared to police as an act of aggression. They were not there to see the events that led up to it. I did not tell them Peter was trying to incite me, threatening to make calls. I masked the situation. Of course, I cannot say for sure if my side of the story would have made a difference in the police' decision; but it certainly would not have hurt.)

o   "If there is any question, if there is any doubt about what is going on in the home," Kardian says, "*reach out*. Make a phone call." Most communities have domestic crisis organizations. Learn what they are. You can also contact RAINN (*www.rainn.org*), which focuses on sexual assault but offers other resources for people suffering in other ways. This kind of pro-action can protect you before you become victim to violence or a set-up.

o   Before you take any action, no matter how the moment strikes you, *do not react*. "Especially when a situation gets heated, the next step is generally physical," says Kardian. "Try your best to regain your senses and go back to the basics, and not reengage in the situation, and avoid physical contact."

o   System-savvy men are the hardest for police to nail. The more experience the perpetrators have negotiating the system, the more experience they have with laws, "the better they are able to pull something off," Kardian notes. "Once they become aware of the system, and what their rights are, they can manipulate their way through." Domestic violence issues are no different. If your husband is legally savvy, you will have to be even more on your guard.

o To further help identify someone capable of system manipulation, Kardian recommends two books by Sandra L. Brown: *How to Spot a Dangerous Man*, and *Women Who Love Psychopaths, Sociopaths, and Narcissists* (see Appendix C for details). Narcissism is a hot-button label these days, Kardian notes, "and it's not anything that's going to go away."

o Intuition. Use it. "Of all the animal species on the earth, the only beings that don't listen to intuition are people," Kardian says. Because women are typically not as big, strong, or aggressive as men, "Women have the greater gift of intuition."

Practical Protection

Eyes for Lies[SM] (*www.eyesforlies.com*) is a nationally recognized professional deception and credibility expert. She is one of only 50 individuals scientists found to spot deception with great accuracy after testing more than 15,000 people, including many law enforcement professionals. She assists law enforcement on homicides and other cases involving deception, and teaches law enforcement how to spot reliable clues to deception in her training courses. She can also review 9-1-1 calls to assist attorneys and police with cues to deception. She is a rare and indispensable tool to authorities.

Eyes for Lies' chief tenet: *Don't brush off red flags.*

o "I think a lot of people who experience this situation are in self denial," she says. "If you're getting a red flag going up, you have to deal with it." Women may be indeed seeing clues; but they're in denial something is wrong. They want to ignore it because it is too painful. When this happens, Eyes says, consider this: Do you want a short term pain (acceptance of the truth) for a long term gain (a healthy relationship), or do you want a long term pain (denying red flags) for a short term gain (forgetting it for a minute)?

o Be vigilant; do not let anything slip. "You have to investigate and not deny any facts you get. It's not being confrontational—you want to be very tactful." For example, if your instincts are pricking up and your spouse says he is going to work late, call the office landline. If he says he's going somewhere, quietly drive by. Is the car there? "You have to thoroughly go through and get the right answer. You have to be honest with yourself. Investigate quietly, get your facts in order, then make a plan."

o Attitude is a huge clue. Eyes' biggest tipoff that someone has a big propensity to be deceptive? Arrogance. "Arrogant people always put themselves before other people," she said. A second attitudinal clue is defensiveness. "Why should someone be defensive—unless they have something to defend, something to hide?"

o To spot deception, you must first know what is true. "True love is always understanding," Eyes says. "If you're not getting understanding, you have to question if you're being loved."

o Clues to deception come in many forms. Don't discount them if you see them:

➢ Liars' emotions won't match their words. For example, they may say they are happy, but give you a fake smile. Learn to identify the difference. You can practice on your own at *http://www.eyesforlies.com/emotions.htm.*

➢ Liars may tell you that they are not angry, but they may leak what is called a micro expression (which occurs in less than the blink of an eye) that tells you they really are. The most dangerous expression of emotion you can see is a combination of disgust and anger, or anger and contempt. It means you are heading for serious trouble.

➢ Liars confuse verb tense when talking about things they didn't actually do, and use present tense instead of past tense (because they are actively thinking as they make up their story, instead of recalling factual details).

➢ Liars often shake their head "yes" when they say "no" (and vice versa). This is very hard to do consciously—try it!

➢ Liars often show clues that they have to think to answer a question, whereas honest people don't—their words just flow naturally.

➢ Liars often use hedge words such as "sort of", "kind of", "maybe", "as if", and "like to" when making a definitive statement. "For example," Eyes says, "one convicted murderer said, 'A lot of my close immediate friends know that I sort of didn't do it.' He *sort of* didn't do it? How is that possible?"

Protecting Your Property

Author's Note: Here are a few more precautionary suggestions, including safeguarding your possessions before they can be separated from you:

o   Secure your own valuables and important papers. You might keep them at a friend's, or rent a safe-deposit box at a nearby bank. Get them out of the house, which quickly becomes a no-holds-barred war zone in a divorce. This includes treasured pictures, children's notes, and so on. Do not burn or shred romantic notes and affectionate cards your spouse gave you in happier times, even though you desperately want to destroy it all. Stash them in a safe place. They state nice, loving things about you and show that you are a good wife and mother. They are important written evidence, especially if your spouse is trying to denigrate you in court.

o   Back up the hard drive of your personal computer, and lock it down, beyond just changing passwords. Protect your property.

o   Be exceptionally wary of how you use email, social media, and so on. Tread delicately in cyberspace. Don't post your divorce developments on Facebook or tweet details—except perhaps to change your marital status after it's all said and done. If it's an adorable photo of you and your children doing something fun, or of you attending a family activity, or the like, fine. Just don't post anything *anywhere* that you wouldn't want the general public to know—including your spouse and your spouse's attorney. Anything that portrays you as anything other than on the total up and up, morally, ethically, and every other way, will weaken your case.

As technology evolves and advances, so will opportunities for entrapment evolve and grow in sophistication. There will be no end. People are, more and more, using electronic communication to set up and spy on one another. Likewise, everything you do online or via texting is traceable. You leave footprints everywhere you go. This includes GPS tracking. Whether or not it is admissible in court, why risk it? Remember to act as if there is a judge watching your every move.

Also, know this: Erasing email and web searches and the like does not delete it from a hard drive—or the hard drive of the recipient. In short, there is no covering up anything conducted online. Electronic set-up tactics and other risks: Don't do it!

o *Keep your hands to yourself.* It sounds glib, but it is not meant to be. Considering keeping your nails short. A scratch appears violent (see Why Does a Scratch Trump a Bruise? above), even if it occurs accidentally or in self defense. All of the scratches in this book were accidental—all of them landed us in jail. No one wants to hurt anybody anyway.

Financial Protection

Women need to gain financial control of their lives in order to protect themselves and their children.

Financial control is the number one tactic that is utilized by batterers, according to Alexis Moore of Survivors in Action (*www.survivorsinaction.org*). "Even the strongest of women realize that without money they have few options," she says. "They need the support of the DV agencies, employers and the public at large to get out. This means that DV organizations must be prepared to assist women with children to find ways to regain financial control and to provide them with the resources needed to become survivors."

Attempts to control finances stem from the abuser's desire to isolate the victim and control her. "Once we begin to assist the victims to gain financial control and provide them with the resources to do so the victim will become a survivor much more quickly," Moore says. "This means that domestic violence institutions of today that receive the funding must be aware, ready, willing and able to assist the victim get back on their feet so that this financial control element is gone."

o   Insist on taking part in the financial decision making. Insist on seeing the bills, the bank statements, and all other financial information. If you do not pay the bills, tell your spouse you want to take over or at least pay them together. If your spouse does not let you, you need to find out what is going on in another way.

   If your spouse has bills and statements sent to his workplace, this might be a significant red flag (unless your spouse's employer needs to see certain bills to reimburse them, as in the case of someone who travels a lot).

o   Establish a bank account in your own name. Keep your bank records safe and private. If you have a job, full or part time, find a way to put aside some extra in your account where you can.

o   Add "found money" to your account. This can include tax refunds, monetary gifts, and other incidental means that show up. It is tempting to want to go spend it on a little vacation, new clothes, or something for the children. Realize this money could be required for your future.

- o If you inherit family money, save it.
- o Take stock of your possessions. Sell those you do not need on consignment, or eBay. Put the money aside.
- o Look for sources of potential income, whether building on a skill you have or starting a small business, and allocate a portion of your earnings to your personal account. Realize you are entitled to keep at least a portion of the money you earn.
- o Keep up professional licenses, skills, associations, and training. Even if you are home full-time, you can maintain your industry contacts and stay current. You might also train and educate yourself for a new profession from home or take evening courses so you are not starting from scratch if you need to quickly get back into the working world.
- o If you feel something is pressing, try to find a way to borrow a sum of money to fall back on if need be. Work out a plan with the lender that would enable you to pay it back over time.

Burning Sage

An Ancient Cleansing Ritual

White sage smudge bundle

Burning sage is one of the oldest and purest methods of cleansing a person, group of people, or space. Saging, commonly known as smudging, is an ancient Native American practice of spiritual cleansing and blessing and involves burning certain dried herbs.

Do not mistake ritual saging for an occult practice. Consider the many civilizations that have utilized sacred herbs and resins in their rituals. There are many references to burning incense in both the Old and New Testaments of the Bible. In some Catholic, Lutheran and Anglican churches, an altar server slowly swings a thurible, a metal censer suspended from chains, as part of the service or Mass.

The early Egyptians regarded the use of incense as central to their worship of the gods. Ancient Indians burned it in purification ceremonies. Hindus use incense for all temple and domestic offerings. Buddhists burn incense as integral parts of festivals, initiations, and daily rites. The Chinese use incense to honor ancestors and household or tutelary deities. In Japan, burning incense is a cornerstone of Shinto ritual. The Orphic Greeks burned incense for protection as early as the 8th century BCE. The Romans considered it an essential element in sacrifices, especially in the worship of the emperor.[45]

Saging For Healing

The Latin word for sage, *Salvia*, derives from the words "to heal." Other qualities of sage when burned are said to include: instilling wisdom; providing clarity; and increasing spiritual awareness.

You can burn sage to purify the energy in your home, office, or any other areas you wish to cleanse. This ceremony is included here especially for those whose homes have been the settings of violence, sadness, and confusion. It is also a nice idea if you move or stay somewhere new. It helps make the living space your own. After a smudging, you may notice a lightness of energy and calmness. The old energy is replaced by fresh new energy and possibilities.

You can burn sage in your living space any time. Some practitioners recommend burning sage once a week to keep the energy clear and positive in the home.

---

[45] "The Fine Art of Smudging." *Incense Warehouse*. N.p., n.d. Web. 3 July 2011. *http://www.incensewarehouse.com/The-Fine-Art-of-Smudging_ep_32-1.html*

Preparing Your Own Saging Ritual

There are many types of sage. The most popular type for smudging is white sage. (You can use dried garden sage too.) You can buy a sage bundle similar to the one pictured above at a local farmer's market or health food store, like Whole Foods. Many online stores carry a wide variety of incense and sage bundles; several are listed below.

You will need a small earthenware pot or bowl (or other heatproof vessel). Place the bundled sage into the pot and light it for a few seconds, letting the smoke billow up. Dry sage will catch fire quickly, so watch your fingers. Some people like to use a long feather to help disperse the smoke.

If you are burning sage to purify a space, or a person (even yourself!), you should first clear your mind as best you can of negative emotions, thoughts, and worries.

Being careful not to breathe in the smoke directly, slowly walk around where you are and take the smoke to each area you would like to clear. Concentrate on "gateway" areas like windows, doors, closets, and hallways. Pay attention to the corners of the room. Use your intuition.

(When we smudged Jessica's home for the first time, our bundle seemed to flare up into a small inferno as we descended her airless basement stairs. It freaked us out a little. Later, a somewhat shaken Jessica told me that the large basement room at the bottom of the stairway was the site of the argument that led to her arrest.)

You may hear a song, hymn or chant bubble up from your subconscious; this is perfectly natural.[46] You can even (carefully) sage your pets and their sleeping areas.

If you want to be especially thorough, you can burn incense immediately after a saging session. Sage is said to have a masculine (yang) aspect, and is complemented by the feminine (yin) aspect of incense.

Here is just a sampling of many sources of saging supplies and incense:

www.annasincense.com

www.incensewarehouse.com

www.juniperridge.com

---

[46] "The art of burning sage." N.p., n.d. Web. 3 July 2011. *piodalcin.wordpress.com/2010/03/31/the-art-of-burning-sage/*.

ஒ

If It Happens To You

I f this happens to you—you are arrested on criminal domestic violence or similar charges, or become victim to other divorce ploys—it is natural to feel abandoned and alone. This book is testimony that nothing can stop you from moving on with your life.

There will be emotional hurdles to clear. It feels terrible to be treated like a criminal or a social pariah, when you feel you have done nothing but try to make a satisfying life for yourself and your family.

People might question: How bad can a short jail stint be? You are not doing hard time, right? If you consider how unthinkable, how foreign, the experience is to most women, and how bad it feels for your own spouse to put you there, we are all here to say, it is pretty darn terrible.

But bear this in mind: This is not the worst thing that can happen. You are safer than you were at home, for reasons that are obvious. When you return home, all the rules may have changed, but you will know to be on your guard and you will know how to get help.

A jail stay on most domestic violence charges is typically brief. Women in this book reported time held from a few hours of booking and immediate release, to a week. For most of us, it was a night, or maybe two or three, if the arrest occurred on a weekend, like mine. There may be a temporary restraining order. Criminal defense attorneys like Tamara Holder specialize in combating this. It is likely you can have your charges dropped.

You will live through it, drawing on the strength you have inside. You can even laugh at the absurdity of it. Jessica and I could barely compare notes on our common experiences without cracking up. It was not exactly so funny, but it was that crazy. Of course, this was years later; it helps when you have a friend who has lived through the same thing, to let you know it is not just you.

Now you have friends. If this thing happens to you, you know it is not just you. Please share this book with anyone you know who needs company and encouragement. Information about ordering additional copies of this book (with a special bulk rate), as well as other titles that may prove helpful in a divorce or difficult relationship, can be found at *www.janiemcqueen.com.*

Light Prayer

I release—

All of my past

All of my negatives

All of my fears

All of my relationships

All of my future

And my inner self

To the LIGHT!

I am a Light being

I radiate the Light from my Light Source to everything

I radiate the Light from my Light Source to every living thing.

I am in a bubble of Light

Only Light can come to me

And only Light surrounds me.

Thank you, God, for

Everything.

Source: I first ran across "Light Prayer" amid papers my grandmother saved for me. She had copied it on the back of an envelope. It is an adaptation of "The Effective Prayer" based on Biblical passages. My grandmother's handwritten "Light Prayer" hangs framed by my back door, where I can see it every day.

❦

"This too shall pass."
—King Solomon

APPENDIX A

Domestic Violence Arrest Policies by State

State	Arrest Stance for Domestic Violence Reports	Circumstances	Coded Relationships [1]
Alabama	DISCRETIONARY Ala. Code § 15-10-3 (a)(8)	An officer may arrest a person without a warrant, on any day and at anytime in any of the following instances: When an offense involves domestic violence as defined by this section, and the arrest is based on probable cause, regardless of whether the offense is a felony or misdemeanor.	
Alaska	MANDATORY Alaska Stat. § 18.65.530(a)	Probable cause to believe that a crime of domestic violence was committed within past 12 hours.	A,B,C,D,E
Arizona	MANDATORY Ariz. Rev. Stat. Ann. § 13-3601(B)	Domestic violence involving infliction of physical injury or use/threatening use deadly weapon.	A, B, C, E
Arkansas	PREFERRED Ark. Code Ann.§ 16-81-113	Preferred action when evidence indicates that domestic abuse has occurred.	

State	Arrest Stance for Domestic Violence Reports	Circumstances	Coded Relationships [1]
California	PREFERRED Cal. Penal Code § 13701 (b)	The written policies shall encourage the arrest of domestic violence offenders if there is probable cause that an offense has been committed.	
Colorado	MANDATORY Colo. Rev. Stat. § 18-6-803.6(1)	Probable cause to believe a crime of domestic violence was committed.	A, B, C
Connecticut	MANDATORY Conn. Gen. Stat. § 46b-38b(a)	Speedy information that family violence was committed in jurisdiction.	A, B, C, E
Delaware	DISCRETIONARY Del. Code Ann. tit.11§1904(a)(4)	Whenever a law enforcement officer has reasonable grounds to believe a person has committed a misdemeanor involving physical injury or the threat thereof or any misdemeanor involving illegal sexual contact or attempted sexual contact.	
District Of Columbia	MANDATORY D.C. Code Ann. § 16-1031	Probable cause to believe that an intrafamily offense was committed that resulted in physical injury	A, B, C, D, E

State	Arrest Stance for Domestic Violence Reports	Circumstances	Coded Relationships [1]
		including pain or illness or caused or was intended to cause reasonable fear of imminent serious physical injury or death.	
Florida	DISCRETIONARY Fla. Stat. ch. 741.29 (3)	Whenever a law enforcement officer determines upon probable cause that an act of domestic violence has been committed within the jurisdiction the officer may arrest the person or persons suspected of its commission and charge such person or persons with the appropriate crime. The decision to arrest and charge shall not require consent of the victim or consideration of the relationship of the parties.	
Georgia	DISCRETIONARY Ga. Code Ann. § 17-4-20 (a)	An arrest for a crime may be made by a law enforcement officer either under a warrant or without a warrant if the offense is committed in such	

State	Arrest Stance for Domestic Violence Reports	Circumstances	Coded Relationships [1]
		officer's presence or within such officer's immediate knowledge if the officer has probable cause to believe that an act of family violence has been committed.	
Hawaii	DISCRETIONARY Haw. Rev. Stat §709-906 (2)	Any police officer, with or without a warrant, may arrest a person if the officer has reasonable grounds to believe that the person is physically abusing, or has physically abused, a family or household member and that the person arrested is guilty thereof.	
Idaho	DISCRETIONARY Idaho Code §19-603 (6)	A peace officer may make an arrest when upon immediate response to a report of a commission of a crime there is probable cause to believe that the person arrested has committed a violation of section 18-902 (assault), 18-903 (battery),18-918 (domestic assault or battery).	
Illinois	DISCRETIONARY	Whenever a law	

State	Arrest Stance for Domestic Violence Reports	Circumstances	Coded Relationships [1]
	725 Ill. Comp. Stat. 5/112A-30	enforcement officer has reason to believe that a person has been abused by a family or household member, the officer shall immediately use all reasonable means to prevent further abuse, including arresting the abusing party, where appropriate.	
Indiana	DISCRETIONARY Ind. Code Ann. § 35-33-1-1 (a)(5)(C)	A law enforcement officer may arrest a person when the officer has probable cause to believe the person has committed a domestic battery under IC 35-42-2-1.3.	
Iowa	MANDATORY Iowa Code § 236.12(2)	Probable cause to believe that domestic abuse assault committed that resulted in bodily injury, or was committed with intent to inflict serious injury, or with use or display of dangerous weapon.	A, B, C, E
Kansas	MANDATORY Kan. Stat. Ann. § 22-2307(b)(1)	Probable cause to believe a crime has been committed.	A,B, C, E

State	Arrest Stance for Domestic Violence Reports	Circumstances	Coded Relationships [1]
Kentucky	DISCRETIONARY Ky. Rev. Stat. Ann. § 431.005(2)(a)	Any peace officer may arrest a person without a warrant when he has probable cause to believe that the person has intentionally or wantonly caused physical injury to a family member or member of an unmarried couple.	
Louisiana	MANDATORY La. Rev. Stat. Ann. § 46:2140 ; Ch. C. Art. 1573(1)	Reason to believe family or household member has been abused and (1) probable cause exists to believe that aggravated/second degree battery was committed or (2) aggravated or simple assault or simple battery committed and reasonable belief in impending danger to abused.	A,B, E
Maine	MANDATORY Me. Rev. Stat. Ann. tit. 19-A, § 4012(5)	Probable cause to believe there has been a violation of title 17-A, section 208 (aggravated assault statute) between members of same family or household.	A, B, C, D, E
Maryland	DISCRETIONARY	A police officer without	

State	Arrest Stance for Domestic Violence Reports	Circumstances	Coded Relationships [1]
	Md. Code Ann. § 2-204	a warrant may arrest a person if (s)he has probable cause to believe that:(i) the person battered the person's spouse or another person with whom the person resides; (ii) there is evidence of physical injury; and, (iii) unless the person is arrested immediately, the person: 1.may not be apprehended; 2.may cause physical injury or property damage to another; or 3. may tamper with, dispose of, or destroy evidence; and a report to the police was made within 48 hours of the alleged incident.	
Massachusetts	PREFERRED Mass. Gen. Laws Ann. ch. 209A § 6 (7)	Preferred response whenever the officer has witnessed or has probable cause to believe that a person has committed a felony, a misdemeanor involving abuse, or an assault and battery.	

State	Arrest Stance for Domestic Violence Reports	Circumstances	Coded Relationships [1]
Michigan	DISCRETIONARY Mich. Comp. Laws § 764.15a	A peace officer may arrest an individual regardless of whether (s)he has a warrant or whether the violation was committed in presence of the peace officer, has or receives positive information that another peace officer has reasonable cause to believe both of the following: (a) The violation occurred or is occurring. (b) The individual has had a child in common with the victim, resides or has resided in the same household as the victim, has or has had a dating relationship with the victim, or is a spouse or former spouse of the victim.	
Minnesota	DISCRETIONARY Minn. Stat. § 629.341 (1)	A peace officer may arrest a person anywhere without a warrant, including at the person's residence, if (s)he has probable cause to believe that within the preceding 12 hours the person has	

State	Arrest Stance for Domestic Violence Reports	Circumstances	Coded Relationships [1]
		committed domestic abuse. The arrest may be made even though the assault did not take place in the presence of the peace officer.	
Mississippi	MANDATORY Miss. Code Ann. § 99-3-7(3)	Probable cause to believe that within 24 hours offender knowingly committed a misdemeanor act of domestic violence.	A, B, E
Missouri	MANDATORY Mo. Rev. Stat. § 455.085	Called to same address within 12 hours and probable cause to believe same offender has committed abuse or assault against same or other family/household member.	A, B, E
Montana	PREFERRED Mont. Code Ann.§ 46-6-311(2)(a)	Preferred response in partner or family member assault cases involving injury to the victim, use or threatened use of a weapon, ... or other imminent danger to the victim.	
Nebraska	DISCRETIONARY Neb. Rev. Stat. § 29-404.02(3)	A peace officer may arrest a person without a warrant if (s) he has	

State	Arrest Stance for Domestic Violence Reports	Circumstances	Coded Relationships [1]
		reasonable cause to believe that such person has committed one or more of the following acts to one or more household members: (a) Attempting to cause or intentionally, knowingly, or recklessly causing bodily injury with or without a deadly weapon; or (b) Threatening another in a menacing manner.	
Nevada	MANDATORY Nev. Rev. Stat. Ann. § 171.137(1)	Probable cause to believe that within 24 hours battery was committed.	A, B, C, D, E
New Hampshire	DISCRETIONARY N.H. Rev. Stat. Ann. § 173-B:9 & N.H. Rev. Stat. Ann. § 594:10 (I)(b)	An arrest for abuse may be made without a warrant upon probable cause, whether or not the abuse is committed in the presence of the peace officer. An arrest by a peace officer without a warrant on a charge of a misdemeanor or a violation is lawful whenever there is probable cause to believe that the person	

State	Arrest Stance for Domestic Violence Reports	Circumstances	Coded Relationships [1]
		to be arrested has within the past 6 hours committed abuse as defined in RSA 173-B:1, I against a person eligible for protection from domestic violence.	
New Jersey	MANDATORY N.J. Stat. Ann. § 2C:25-21(a)	Probable cause to believe that domestic violence has occurred and either victim shows signs of injury or probable cause that a weapon was involved.	A, B, C, D, E
New Mexico	DISCRETIONARY N.M. Stat. Ann§ 40-13-7 (B)(5)	A local law enforcement officer responding to the request for assistance shall be required to take whatever steps are reasonably necessary to protect the victim from further domestic abuse, including: arresting the abusing household member when appropriate and including a written statement in the attendant police report to indicate that the arrest of the abusing household member was,	

State	Arrest Stance for Domestic Violence Reports	Circumstances	Coded Relationships [1]
		in whole or in part, premised upon probable cause to believe that the abusing household member committed domestic abuse against the victim.	
New York	MANDATORY N.Y. Crim. Proc. Law § 140.10(4)(a)	Probable cause to believe a felony has been committed against a member of the same family or household or, unless victim requests otherwise, a misdemeanor family offense committed.	A, C, E
North Carolina	DISCRETIONARY NC Gen. Stat. § 15A-401 (b)(2)	An officer may arrest without a warrant any person whom (s)he has probable cause to believe has committed a misdemeanor, *and* will not be apprehended unless immediately arrested, *or* may cause physical injury to himself or others, or damage to property unless immediately arrested, or has committed one of the following (listed) misdemeanors.	

State	Arrest Stance for Domestic Violence Reports	Circumstances	Coded Relationships [1]
North Dakota	DISCRETIONARY N.D. Cent. Code § 14-07.1-10(1)	If probable cause to believe that a person has committed a crime involving domestic violence, whether the offense is a felony or misdemeanor, and whether or not the crime was committed in the presence of the officer, then the law enforcement officer shall presume that arresting the person is the appropriate response.	
Ohio	MANDATORY Ohio Rev. Code Ann. § 2935.032(A)(1)(a)(i)	Reasonable cause to believe that offender committed felonious assault.	A,B.C, E
Oklahoma	DISCRETIONARY Okla. Stat. tit. 22, § 40.3 (B)	A peace officer may arrest without a warrant a person anywhere, including his place of residence, if the peace officer has probable cause to believe the person within the preceding seventy-two (72) hours has committed an act of domestic abuse as defined by Section	

State	Arrest Stance for Domestic Violence Reports	Circumstances	Coded Relationships [1]
		60.1of this title, although the assault did not take place in the presence of the peace officer. Officer must observe a recent physical injury to, or an impairment of the physical condition of, the alleged victim.	
Oregon	MANDATORY Or. Rev. Stat. § 133.055(2)(a)	Probable cause to believe that a felonious assault or an assault resulting in injury occurred or action has placed another to reasonably fear imminent serious bodily injury or death.	A, B, C, D, E
Pennsylvania	DISCRETIONARY 18 Pa. Cons. Stat. § 2711(A)	A police officer shall have the same right of arrest without a warrant as in a felony whenever (s)he has probable cause to believe the defendant has violated section 2504 (relating to involuntary manslaughter), 2701 (relating to simple assault), 2702(a)(3), (4) and (5) (relating to	

State	Arrest Stance for Domestic Violence Reports	Circumstances	Coded Relationships [1]
		aggravated assault), 2705 (relating to recklessly endangering another person), 2706 (relating to terroristic threats) or 2709(b) (relating to harassment and stalking) against a family or household member although the offense did not take place in the presence of the police officer. An officer may not arrest a person pursuant to this section without first observing recent physical injury to the victim or other corroborative evidence.	
Rhode Island	MANDATORY R.I. Gen. Laws § 12-29-3(c)(1)	Probable cause to believe the following: felonious assault: assault resulting in injury: action was intended to cause fear of imminent serious bodily injury or death.	A, B, C, D, E
South Carolina	MANDATORY S.C. Code Ann. § 16-25-70(B)	If physical injury is present and probable cause to believe person is committing or has freshly committed a	A, B, C, E

State	Arrest Stance for Domestic Violence Reports	Circumstances	Coded Relationships [1]
		misdemeanor/felony assault or battery.	
South Dakota	MANDATORY S.D. Codified Laws § 23A-3-2.1	Probable cause to believe that within previous 4 hours [2], there has been an aggravated assault, an assault resulting in bodily injury, or an attempt by physical menace to place in fear of imminent serious bodily injury.	A, B, C, E
Tennessee	PREFERRED Tenn. Code Ann.§ 36-3-619	Preferred response when probable cause to believe that a crime committed involving domestic abuse within or outside presence of the office	
Texas	DISCRETIONARY Tex. Code Crim. P. Ann. art. 14.03 (a)(4)	Any peace officer may arrest, without a warrant persons whom the peace officer has probable cause to believe have committed an assault resulting in bodily injury to a member of the person's family or household.	
Utah	MANDATORY Utah Code Ann. § 77-	Probable cause to believe that an act of	A, B, C, E

State	Arrest Stance for Domestic Violence Reports	Circumstances	Coded Relationships [1]
	36-2.2(2)(a)	domestic violence was committed and there will be continued violence or evidence perpetrator has recently caused serious bodily injury or used a dangerous weapon.	
Vermont	DISCRETIONARY Vt .R. Cr. P. 3(a)(C)	An officer may also arrest a person without warrant in the following situations: that a person has committed a misdemeanor which involves an assault against a family member, or against a household member as defined in 15 V.S.A. § 1101(2), or a child of such a family or household member.	
Virginia	MANDATORY Va. Code Ann. § 19.2-81.3(B)	Probable cause to believe assault or battery on family or household member.	A, B, C, E
Washington	MANDATORY Wash. Rev. Code § 10.31.100(2)(c)	Probable cause to believe a person 16 years or older within the previous 4 hours assaulted a family or household member and	A, B, C, D, E

State	Arrest Stance for Domestic Violence Reports	Circumstances	Coded Relationships [1]
		believes (1) felonious assault occurred, or (2) assault resulting in bodily injury occurred whether injury is visible or not, or (3) any physical action occurred which was intended to cause reasonable fear of imminent serious bodily injury or death.	
West Virginia	DISCRETIONARY W.Va. Code § 48-27-1002(a)	A law-enforcement officer has authority to arrest that person without first obtaining a warrant if (s)he has observed credible corroborative evidence that an offense has occurred *and* either the law-enforcement officer has received, from the victim or a witness, an oral or written allegation of facts constituting a violation of section twenty-eight, article two, chapter sixty-one of this code (domestic violence offense) or the law-enforcement officer has observed credible evidence that the	

State	Arrest Stance for Domestic Violence Reports	Circumstances	Coded Relationships [1]
		accused committed the offense.	
Wisconsin	MANDATORY Wis. Stat. § 968.075 (2)(a)	Reasonable cause to believe that offender committing or has committed domestic abuse and either evidence of physical injury or reasonable basis for believing continued abuse is likely.	A, B, E
Wyoming	DISCRETIONARY Wyo. Stat. Ann. § 7-20-102 (a)	In addition to arrests specified in W.S. 7-2-102, any peace officer who has probable cause to believe that a violation of W.S. 6-2-501(a), (b), (e) or (f), 6-2-502(a) or 6-2-504(a) or (b) has taken place within the preceding twenty-four (24)hours or is taking place and that the person who committed or is committing the violation is a household member as defined by W.S. 35-21-102(a)(iv), may arrest the violator without a warrant for that violation,	

State	Arrest Stance for Domestic Violence Reports	Circumstances	Coded Relationships [1]
		regardless of whether the violation was committed in the presence of the peace officer.	

[1] Coded Relationships: (A) current/former spouse, (B) current/former cohabitant, (C) child in common, (D) dating relationship,(E) related by marriage or blood

[2] Amended in 2001 to 24 hour

Source: Hirschel, David. "Domestic Violence Cases: What Research Shows About Arrest and Dual Arrest Rates | National Institute of Justice." *National Institute of Justice: Criminal Justice Research, Development and Evaluation.* N.p., 25 July 2008. Web. 24 June 2011. Note: Laws are constantly changing. Be sure to check your state statutes to ensure up-to-date information.

APPENDIX B

States that Allow Expungement

Each state has its own specific laws regarding which types of crimes, if any, are eligible for expungement. Some states forbid expungement or sealing of records for domestic violence *convictions*—such as Colorado, Florida, Texas, and Washington state—but most provide some sort of erasure for cases in which DV charges were dropped.

Many types of misdemeanors can be expunged, but generally felony convictions are more difficult to get off your record. The table below provides a brief overview of the laws pertaining to misdemeanor and felony offenses:

State	Felony Expungement	Misdemeanor Expungement
Alabama	Does not allow for expungement. Alabama Section 15-22-36 allows the Board of Pardons and Paroles to grant a pardon or parole except in treason or impeachment cases.	Alabama Section 41-9-625 allows arrest records to be expunged if the charges are not filed, dropped or no conviction is obtained.
Alaska	Alaska Section 12.62.180 allows records to be sealed only if the conviction was due to mistaken identity or false accusation.	Alaska Section 12.62.190 allows the purging of criminal justice information by an agency responsible for maintaining the records if the subject died or the information is no longer relevant.*
Arizona	Arizona Revised Statute ARS 13-907 allows a person to submit a setting aside judgment request to the	A person can submit a setting aside judgment request to the authority that imposed the conviction. Crimes not eligible to be set aside:

authority that imposed the conviction.
Certain crimes are not eligible. See Misdemeanors.
Convicted felons may apply to have their civil rights restored at the end of their probation term.

- o Crimes involving the infliction of serious physical injury to another person
  - o Sex crimes
- o Crimes against children under age 15
- o A moving violation if the defendant's license was suspended or revoked

Arkansas	A felony conviction can be expunged if the person was under age 26 at the time and had no more than one prior felony conviction and the prior felony was not a capital offense, first- or second-degree murder, first-degree rape, kidnapping or aggravated robbery. A person who was convicted of a non-violent felony committed while under age 18, Ark. Code Ann. 16-90-602. Pardoned criminals with the exception of those pardoned for committing offenses against minors, offenses resulting in serious injury, or death and sex offenses, Ark. Code Ann. 16-90-605.	First-time offenders in DUI cases who successfully complete terms of probation, Ark. Code Ann §5-65-108, Ark. Code Ann §5-65-308, Ark. Code Ann §5-64-407. Any person who successfully completes probation or a commitment to the Dept. of Corrections with judicial transfer to the Dept. of Community Corrections for certain offenses that are eligible for community punishment.
California	California Penal Code 1203.4 permits expungement for certain offenses if probation has been completed and they are not charged with any other offense.	Expungement if probation has been completed or one year has passed if it was a low-level misdemeanor.

Colorado	Colorado Rev. Stat. 24-72-308 A person can petition to have arrest and criminal records sealed if they were not charged with a crime, they were acquitted, the case was dismissed or the case was dismissed due to a plea agreement in a separate case.	Misdemeanor DUI offenses, traffic offenses, domestic violence offenses or unlawful sexual behavior offenses are not eligible to be sealed. Records cannot be sealed if the person pled or was found guilty of the offense.
Connecticut	Connecticut General Statutes 54-142a states that records can be expunged if the person has been acquitted, pardoned or the charges were dropped.	Connecticut General Statutes 54-142a states that records cannot be destroyed until three years have elapsed from the date of final disposition of the case.
Delaware	Delaware Code 4372 allows expungement only if the person was acquitted, the prosecutor chooses not to prosecute the case or the court dismissed the case.	Arrest records can be expunged if the case was dismissed or they were found not guilty, except if they were charged with a sex offense, unlawful imprisonment, interference with child custody, trespassing with intent to peep or child endangerment.
District of Columbia	D.C. Code 16-801 allows expungement of a single felony which is a violation of the Bail Reform Act.	D.C. Code 16-801 allows non-serious misdemeanor convictions to be sealed if two years have passed since the case was terminated.
Florida	A felony arrest record can be expunged if the case was dismissed, the charging document was not issued or the prosecutor decides not to prosecute the case. Certain sexual crimes or crimes involving children are ineligible.	A misdemeanor arrest record can

	If the case is prosecuted and the court orders adjudication withheld, expungement may be possible if probation was successfully completed. The individual must petition the court to seal the records and they must be sealed for 10 years before filing for expungement. Florida Statutes Section 943.0585.	be expunged if the case was dismissed, the charging document was not issued or the prosecutor decides not to prosecute the case. Certain misdemeanor arrests are ineligible for expungement including voyeurism, fraud, sex crimes and crimes against children. Florida Statutes Section 943.059.
Georgia	Georgia Code 42-8-60 allows a felony arrest to be expunged if there is no adjudication of guilt and the person has not previously been convicted of a felony offense.	Georgia Statute 35-3-37 allows a criminal arrest record to be expunged if the case was dismissed, the person has no other pending criminal charges and has not previously been convicted of the same or similar offense within the last five years.
Hawaii	Hawaii Statute 831-3.2 allows for expungement of a felony arrest where a conviction has not been obtained.	Hawaii Statute 706.622.5 allows expungement for first-time drug offenders if they complete treatment and probation.
Idaho	Idaho Code 67-3004 allows arrest records to be expunged if the person was not charged, indicted or was acquitted.	A person convicted of a single minor offense can file a petition for expungement of their arrest records.
Illinois	Under the Criminal Identification Act, qualifying arrests, supervisions and convictions can either be expunged or sealed. Felony charges cannot be expunged with the exception of some	Certain misdemeanor offenses are not eligible for expungement: DUI, reckless driving and moving violations for professional drivers. Criminal records can be expunged if the defendant was found not guilty or the offense was not prosecuted.

	felony drug possession or prostitution offenses.	
Indiana	Indiana Code 35-38-5-1 allows expungement of arrest records if the wrong person was arrested, no probable cause for arrest existed, or charges were never file or dropped.	A person can petition the State Police Department to limit access to their criminal history. This applies to the last crime they were convicted of only if 15 years have passed from the date the person was discharged from probation, imprisonment or parole.
Iowa	Iowa Statute 692-17 allows any arrest records to be expunged if the person was acquitted or the charges were dismissed. Iowa Statute 907.9 allows a conviction to be expunged if the court placed the person on probation or they were given a deferred judgment.	Iowa Code Chapters 123.46 and 123.47 requires courts to expunge a prior conviction for minor in possession of alcohol after two years from the conviction date if the person has not been convicted of any other offenses.
Kansas	Kansas Statute 21-4619 allows expungement of Class D or Class E felony convictions, arrest records and diversion agreements.	Kansas Statute 21-4619 allows misdemeanor convictions, arrest records and diversion agreements to be expunged if three or more years have elapsed.
Kentucky	Kentucky Statute 431.076 allows arrest records to be expunged if the charges were dismissed with prejudice or the person has been found not guilty of the charge and has no current charges pending against them.	Misdemeanor convictions may be expunged if five years has passed since their sentence or probation was completed and they do not have a prior felony conviction. Sex crimes and crimes against children are not eligible.
Louisiana	Louisiana Article 893 of the Code of Criminal Procedure gives the court discretion to suspend a sentence in felony	LSA-R.S. 44:9 allows a person charged with a misdemeanor to have their arrest record expunged if the statute of limitations has expired for prosecuting the offense

	cases and place the person on probation. The court can set aside the conviction if probation has been successfully completed.	or the charges were dismissed.
Maine	Maine Statute 611 through 623 allows criminal records to be sealed if there was no conviction, the district attorney declines to prosecute or the charges were dismissed.	An expungement for a misdemeanor is possible through a pardon from the Maine Pardon Board. Maine Statute 2167 allows those granted a pardon to apply for expungement after 10 years has passed.
Maryland	Maryland Code of Criminal Procedure 10-103 allows expungement of a police record if no charges were filed.	Maryland Code of Criminal Procedure 10-105 allows people who are charged with committing a crime to file for expungement upon acquittal or if the charges were dismissed.
Massachusetts	G.L.c.276 100C contains provisions for sealing adult records in cases where the charges were dismissed or the person was acquitted.	G.L.c.276 100A allows adult records to be sealed after a 10 to 15 year waiting period.
Michigan	Michigan Section 780.621 allows one felony conviction to be set aside as long as the offense is not punishable by a term of life in prison.	Michigan Section 780.621 allows a criminal conviction to be set aside if the offense was not a traffic offense, sex crime, felony or attempted felony punishable by life in prison.
Minnesota	Minnesota Statutes Section 299c.11 allows arrest records to be expunged if the charges were dismissed or the prosecutor declines to prosecute the case and the person was not convicted of a	Minnesota Statutes Section 299c.11 allows arrest records to be expunged if the charges were dismissed or the prosecutor declines to prosecute the case.

	felony or gross misdemeanor in the 10 years preceding their arrest.	
Mississippi	Mississippi allows certain felony offenses to be expunged after five years of completing sentence or probation: Bad check offense—Sec. 97-19-55 Possession of controlled substance or paraphernalia—Sec. 41-29-139 False pretense—Sec. 97-17-41 Malicious mischief—Sec. 97-17-67 Shoplifting—Sec. 97-23-93	Section 99-19-71 allows misdemeanor convictions to be expunged for first-time offenders, excluding traffic violations and DUI offenses. Arrest records can be expunged under Section 99-19-71(4) if the case was dismissed or charges were dropped.
Missouri	Missouri Statutes Section 610-122 allows arrest records to be expunged if there was no probable cause for the arrest, charges were dismissed, the arrest was based on false information, the prosecutor declines to prosecute, the suspect has no prior misdemeanor or felony convictions, and there is no civil action pending related to the arrest.	Missouri Statute 577.054.1 allows a conviction for driving while intoxicated (DWI) to be expunged if it was a first offense and charged as a misdemeanor rather than a felony offense. The DWI charge must be at least 10 years old and the individual cannot have any subsequent alcohol related charges or offenses.
Montana	Montana Statute 46-23-510 allows a juvenile or adult to seek expungement who was convicted of a violent or sexual offense, if the case was	The court may defer imposing a sentence for 1 to 3 years for first-time offenders who will remain on probation during that time. Upon successful completion of the diversion program, the charges

	later reversed.	will be dismissed.
Nebraska	Nebraska Article IV, Section 13 allows an individual to apply for a pardon from the Nebraska Board of Pardons. If granted, convicted felons can have their civil rights restored.	Nebraska Statute 29-3523 allows arrest records to be expunged if the arrest was made in error by the law enforcement agency.
Nevada	Nevada Revised Statute 176A.850 allows records to be sealed if the person fulfilled the terms of probation. If they are honorably discharged from probation, their civil rights will be restored. NRS 179-255 allows records to be sealed if the case is dismissed or the defendant is acquitted.	Nevada Revised Statute 176A.265 allows records to be sealed after a defendant is discharged from probation pursuant to NRS 176A.260. NRS 179-259 allows records to be sealed after completion of a reentry program.
New Hampshire	New Hampshire Revised Statute 651:5—A person may petition to have their arrest record annulled if they were acquitted, the charges were dismissed or not prosecuted.	New Hampshire Revised Statute 651:5 allows a person to petition for annulment of arrest and conviction records after completing all the terms and conditions of their sentence.
New Jersey	New Jersey Statute 2C:52-2 allows expungement of arrest and conviction records after a period of 5 years has passed and the person has satisfactorily completed probation or parole who has not been convicted of any prior or subsequent offense within New Jersey or any	New Jersey Statute 2C:52-6 allows expungement of arrest records if charges were dismissed or the person was acquitted.

	other jurisdiction.	
New Mexico	New Mexico Statute 30-31-28 allows first-time drug offenders under age 18 to have arrest records expunged if the charges were dismissed. New Mexico Statute 31-21-17 allows individuals to request a pardon.	New Mexico Statute 29-3-8.1(A) allows a person to expunge arrest records for misdemeanor, petty misdemeanors and crimes not considered to be of moral turpitude.
New York	New York Criminal Procedure Section 160.50 allows arrest records to be sealed if the district attorney decides to terminate criminal proceedings.	New York Criminal Procedure Section 160.58 allows arrest and conviction records to be sealed if the person successfully completes a judicial drug diversion program.
North Carolina	North Carolina Section 15A-146 allows individuals charged with a misdemeanor or felony to expunge their records if the charges were dismissed or the person was acquitted.	North Carolina Section 15A-145 allows all records to be sealed for a misdemeanor conviction other than a traffic violation if the offense was committed before the person turned 18 and they have no prior misdemeanor or felony convictions. An expungement petition can be filed two years after conviction date.
North Dakota	North Dakota Statute 31-13-07 allows a person to seal their DNA evidence if they have not been charged with a felony for at least a year or the case has been dismissed.	North Dakota Statute 19-03.1-23 allows a person to apply for expungement if they were convicted of possession of one ounce or less of marijuana.
Ohio	Ohio Revised Section 2953.61 allows first-time convicted offenders to apply for their	Ohio Revised Section 2953.61 allows first-time convicted offenders to apply for their records to be sealed one year from the date

	records to be sealed three years from the date of their felony conviction.	of their misdemeanor conviction.
Oklahoma	Title 22 of the Oklahoma Statute 991c allows for the expungement of a plea of guilty or no contest after the successful completion of a deferred sentence. The case will be dismissed and court records may be sealed.	Title 22 of the Oklahoma Statute 18 and 19 allows expungement of arrest records if the defendant was acquitted, the conviction was reversed, the statute of limitations expired, the defendant was under 18 at the time, the offense was a misdemeanor and the person has no other convictions or pending criminal cases. At least 10 years must have passed since judgment was entered or the offense was a non-violent felony as defined in Title 57 O.S. 571.
Oregon	Oregon Statute 137.225 allows Class C felonies and felonies treated as a misdemeanor to be set aside, except for sex offenses or those involving child abuse. The conviction can be sealed for one offense three years after the judgment was entered and probation is complete.	Oregon Statute 137.225 allows arrest records to be set aside after a one-year waiting period if the case was dismissed or the defendant was acquitted. The person cannot have been arrested for any other charges within the past 3 years or convicted of any offense within the past 10 years.
Pennsylvania	Pennsylvania Consolidated Statutes 18 Pa.C.S.A. 9122 allows criminal records to be expunged if there is no disposition in the case within 18 months after the arrest date.	Pennsylvania Consolidated Statutes 18 Pa.C.S.A. 9122 allows people 21 years or older convicted of violation of section 6308 relating to the purchase, consumption, possession or transportation of liquor or malt brewed beverages to seek expungement if they have satisfied all the terms of the sentence imposed.
Rhode Island	Rhode Island General Law 12-1.3-2 allows expungement for	Rhode Island General Law 12-1.3-2 allows expungement for first-time offenders who are convicted in

	first-time offenders who are convicted in crimes not involving violence. A person can file for expungement if convicted of a felony offense if 10 years has passed with no further criminal arrests or convictions.	crimes not involving violence. A person can file for expungement if convicted of a misdemeanor offense if 5 years has passed with no further criminal arrests or convictions. Rhode Island General Law 12-1-12.1 allows arrest and court records to be sealed for defendants who are acquitted or no charges were filed, and if they were not convicted of a prior felony offense.
South Carolina	Section 34-11-90 allows records to be sealed if the defendant was convicted under the Fraudulent Check Law and no additional criminal activity has taken place for one year from the conviction date. Section 44-53-450 allows records to be sealed if charges were dismissed and the offense did not involve a Schedule I or Schedule II controlled substance. Section 22-5-920 allows records to be sealed for a first time conviction as a youthful offender after the defendant has completed the terms of their probation or parole. They can apply after 5 years from the conviction date.	Section 17-1-40 allows records to be expunged if the charge was dismissed, not prosecuted or the defendant was acquitted. Section 17-22-150 allows records to be sealed if the defendant successfully completes a pre-trial intervention program, alcohol or traffic education program. Section 22-5-910 allows records to be sealed for a first conviction if the crime carries a penalty of no more than 30 days in jail or a fine of $500. Section 56-5-750 allows records to be sealed if the defendant was convicted for a first non-aggravated violation for "Failure to Stop for a Blue Light and Siren" and had no other convictions within three years.
South Dakota	South Dakota Codified Law 23-6-8.1 allows the destruction of criminal	South Dakota Codified Law 23A-27-17 allows the sealing of records for certain convictions after probation

	records if:	has been completed.
	○ The offense is no longer considered a crime ○ The person is 75 years or older and has not had a violation within the last 10 years ○ The person is dead	South Dakota Codified Law 23-6-8.1 allows the destruction of criminal records if the misdemeanor offense occurred at least 10 years prior.
Tennessee	TCA 40-35-313 allows records to be sealed if the charges were dismissed, no indictment was returned by a grand jury, the defendant was acquitted or no charges were filed after an arrest. Sexual offenses are not eligible.	TCA 40-32-101 allows a first-time offender to have their records sealed if they were under age 21 and it was not a sexual offense.
Texas	Article 55.02 allows for expungement if the defendant was acquitted, convicted and subsequently pardoned, the statute of limitations expired or a felony indictment was not returned by a grand jury.	Individuals convicted under Section 161.252 may apply to have the conviction expunged if the individual completed the tobacco awareness program or tobacco-related community service. Records relating to misdemeanor charges for chemical dependency may be expunged under Article 55.01.
Utah	The State of Utah allows expungement of an arrest if the person has not more than one felony or two Class A misdemeanor convictions. Utah Statute 77-18-11 allows a person convicted of a crime to	An expungement may be obtained if the charges were dismissed, never filed, the defendant was acquitted or they have been released from jail, probation or parole. Utah Statute 77-18-10 allows petition of expungement if at least 30 days has passed since

	petition the court for an expungement of their record.	the arrest.
Vermont	Under 5413, a person who is convicted of a sex offense that is reversed and dismissed will have their records removed and they will not be required to register as a convicted sex offender.	Under 33 V.S.A. 7041, when criminal proceedings are discharged and restitution is fully paid, an expungement will be granted.
Virginia	Code of Virginia Statute 19.2-392.2 allows a person charged with a crime to have their records expunged if they are acquitted, granted an absolute pardon if unjustly convicted or the prosecution does not pursue the case.	Code of Virginia Statute 19.2-392.2 allows a person to have their record expunged if their name or other identification was used by another person without their consent or authorization by a person charged with a crime.
Washington	RCS 46.61.502(6) or 46.61.504(6) allows Washington State Class B and Class C felony offenses to be expunged if it was not a sexual offense. Class C after 10 years and Class B after 5 years.	Under RCW 9.96, a domestic violence misdemeanor conviction can be expunged after 5 years, misdemeanor after 3 years and gross misdemeanors or deferred misdemeanors after 2 years.
West Virginia	West Virginia Code 5-1-16a allows anyone who has received a full pardon from the governor to petition the court for expungement. West Virginia Code 60A-4-407 allows a conditional discharge for a first offense of drug possession if no prior convictions exists.	West Virginia Code 61-11-25 allows any person charged with a criminal offense who was acquitted or the charges were dismissed to have all the records expunged. West Virginia Code 61-11-26 allows expungement of misdemeanor offenses committed when the person was between the ages of 18 and 26.

Wisconsin	Wisconsin Statute 973-015 allows certain felony convictions to be expunged if the individual was less than 25 years old at the time and the sentence imposed was for less than 6 years. They must have successfully completed the terms of their sentence and not pose a risk to society.	Wisconsin Statutes 973.015 allows misdemeanor convictions to be expunged if the person completed their sentence successfully and they have not been convicted of another criminal offense since their conviction.
Wyoming	Wyoming Statutes 14-6-241 allows expungement of a juvenile convicted of a non-violent offense if they have reached the age of majority and have not been convicted of a felony since adjudication, and no felony is pending against them.	Wyoming Statutes 7-13-1401 allows expungement when 180 days have passed since the arrest or charges were dismissed.

Source: *www.criminaldefenselawyer.com*

*The state of Alaska will consider "sealing" a record, in which case the petitioner submits a written request, to the head of the agency responsible for maintaining information, asking the agency to seal such information that may have resulted from a false accusation.—Alaska Public Safety Statewide Services

People who want to have their records sealed or expunged should contact a criminal defense attorney in their state of residence. It may be possible to have some records permanently removed so that prospective employers do not have access to them. An experienced attorney can also help convicted felons get their Constitutional rights restored in certain case. For state-specific information on criminal records and expungement visit: *http://criminal.findlaw.com/crimes/expungement/expungement-state-info.html*

APPENDIX C
FURTHER READING AND RESOURCES
BOOKS

Why Does He Do That?: Inside the Minds of Angry and Controlling Men. Lundy Bancroft. New York: Putnam's Sons, 2002. *www.lundybancroft.com*

How to Spot a Dangerous Man Before You Get Involved. Sandra L. Brown. Alameda, Calif: Hunter House, 2005.

Women Who Love Psychopaths, Sociopaths, and Narcissists. Sandra L. Brown and Liane J. Leedom. Health & Wellbeing Publications, 2008.

You Can Heal Your Life. Louise L. Hay. Santa Monica, CA: Hay House, 1987. Also available on audio at *www.louisehay.com*

Orange is the New Black: My Year in a Women's Prison. Piper Kerman. New York: Spiegel & Grau, 2010.

A World Apart: Women, Prison, and Life Behind Bars. Cristina Rathbone. New York: Random House, 2005.

"Not To People Like Us": Hidden Abuse in Upscale Marriages. Susan Weitzman. New York: Basic Books, 2000.

A Safe Place for Women: Surviving Domestic Abuse and Creating a Successful Future. Kelly White. Alameda, Calif: Hunter House, 2010.

WEBSITES

www.aardvarc.org An Abuse, Rape & Domestic Violence Aid & Resource Collection—Extensive, resource-rich website

www.DVReform.org Website promoting DV reform to ensure all victims are afforded equal protections and services regardless of race, gender, sexual orientation, age, and perpetrator's occupation.

www.girlfriendology.com Blog offering general resources for women, and support for friendships.

www.heal-post-traumatic-stress.com Articles and practical resources about living with PTSD

www.justicewomen.com

www.rainn.org The nation's largest anti-sexual violence organization.

www.survivorsinaction.org

www.theanneboleynfiles.com/free-report "The Fall of Anne Boleyn—The Most Happy" King Henry VIII of England sent spirited second wife Anne Boleyn to the Tower of London, the Biggest of Big Houses, in arguably one of the most intricate and outrageous marital set-ups of all time. She held up her head until the very end; and her daughter became one of history's greatest queens, Elizabeth 1.

ARTICLES

Supporting Separated Fathers and Encouraging Men's Positive Involvement in Parenting. Michael Flood. *The Field of Fatherhood: Crossings of the Terrain*, Conference, Hawke Institute for Sustainable Societies, University of South Australia, June 19, 2007.
http://www.unisa.edu.au/hawkeinstitute/documents/SeparatedFathers.pdf

"Paper Abuse": When All Else Fails, Batterers Use Procedural Stalking: Miller, Susan L. Miller, Nicole L. Smolter. Published: *Violence Against Women* . N.p., n.d. Web. 4 July 2011.
http://vaw.sagepub.com/content/17/5/637.abstract?rss=1>.

Victim-Defendants: An Emerging Challenge in Responding to Domestic Violence in Seattle and the King County Region: Meg Crager, Merril Cousin, Tara Hardy Published: April 2003 Copyright © 2001 King County Coalition Against Domestic Violence)
http://www.mincava.umn.edu/documents/victimdefendant/victimdefendant.ht ml

Who Does What to Whom? Gender and Domestic Violence Perpetrators. Hester, M. et al. Bristol: University of Bristol in association with the Northern Rock Foundation 2009
http://www.bristol.ac.uk/sps/research/projects/reports/2009/rj4843/whodoeswh at.pdf

The Protection Battered Spouses Don't Need - New York Times. Radha Iyengar. *The New York Times - Breaking News, World News & Multimedia*. N.p., 7 Aug. 2007. Web. 4 July 2011.
http://www.nytimes.com/2007/08/07/opinion/07iyengar.html

Arresting Developments: Trends in Female Arrests for Domestic Violence and Proposed Explanations. William DeLeon-Granados, William Wells and

Ruddyard Binsbacher. Violence Against Women, Volume 12 Number 4 April 2006 355-371 Sage Publications, 2006. *vaw.sagepub.com*

REPORTS

National Center on Full Faith and Credit. "State Statutes: Misdemeanor Crimes of Domestic Violence." *www.americanbar.org.* Battered Women's Justice Project, n.d. Web. 4 July 2011. *http://www.americanbar.org/content/dam/aba/migrated/domviol/docs/State_ MCDV_Matrix.authcheckdam.pdf*

Effectiveness of Grant Programs under the Violence Against Women Act, 2010 Report to Congress http://muskie.usm.maine.edu/vawamei/attachments/congressreports/ Discretionary2010ReportToCongress.pdf

OVA Grant Awards by State and Program *http://www.ovw.usdoj.gov/grantactivities.htm*

VAWA Measuring Effectiveness Initiative's website at *http://muskie.usm.maine.edu/vawamei/index.htm* .

Arrest Program Progress Report Form Sample—An example of the types of data OVW collects regarding law enforcement activities *(http://muskie.usm.maine.edu/vawamei/attachments/forms/CDSArrestFormGM SSample.pdf)*

ACKNOWLEDGMENTS

This book would never have come into being without the abundant input, encouragement, and support of the following people: my husband Josh, for his unfailing support; Randy Kessler, for his legal insights and constant belief that this book was important; Tamara Holder, for penning a smashing foreword and answering random questions on weekend mornings; Eyes for Lies[SM] and Steve Kardian, for generously sharing their expertise; Mary Patrick, for her excellent editing skills and for making the "new life" possible; Jessica, without whom I would not have had the opportunity to compare notes in the first place; Nichole Bazemore, a constant cheerleader and font of positivity; Alexis Moore, Bonnie Russell, and Jeffrey Smallwood, early responders to my HARO queries and fine sources; Marie DeSantis, for granting me permission to quote abundantly from her info-rich website; Aubry Ballard, for early manuscript reading and being a stunning example of strength in a very public trial; HARO (*www.helpareporter.com*), for helping me locate the perfect sources; Robin Hall, for always being there; beta readers Sarah Chamberlain, Brooke Erwin, Karen Jaggi, Danielle King, Lora King, Sharon Laidlaw, Debbie Maston, and Lisa Perry, for taking time in their busy days to read my manuscript from its roughest drafts and offering thoughtful and helpful suggestions that made all the difference; Jill Buckner, for her time and inspired photos; Haley Bossert, for her beauty and extraordinary composure being photographed in bare feet and handcuffs; Jodi Verbeek, for making a cover design about jail and scratches look as beautiful as the sources herein deserve; and most of all, the intelligent and resilient women and men who trusted me with their stories.

About the Author

Janie McQueen's writing career includes news beats at major metro newspapers including *The Greenville (SC) News* and the *Atlanta Journal-Constitution*, and a stint as a speechwriter for the government of Taiwan during the 1996 Summer Olympics in Atlanta. She is the author of three previous books, including *The Magic Bookshelf*, a parents' favorite and library staple that has also been used in college elementary education classes. The guide, recently released as *The New Magic Bookshelf* in a 10th Anniversary edition, was featured in *Parenting's Babytalk* magazine and as a series in the *Los Angeles Times Book Review* as part of Reading by 9, a literacy initiative. A native of Beaufort, SC, McQueen has a BA in English literature and writing from the University of South Carolina. She is married and the mother of four children, who range in age from 3 to 14. They live in metro Atlanta.

AUTHOR APPEARANCES

Janie McQueen is a popular media guest and speaker. She welcomes interviews and speaking engagements with interested groups. Please visit *www.janiemcqueen.com* for upcoming appearances and contact and booking information.

INDEX